Many Children Left Behind

WITHDRAWN

MANY CHILDREN LEFT BEHIND

How the No Child Left Behind
Act Is Damaging Our Children
and Our Schools

**Edited by Deborah Meier
and George Wood**

BEACON
I50

Beacon Press, Boston

BEACON PRESS
25 Beacon Street
Boston, Massachusetts 02108-2892
www.beacon.org

Beacon Press books are published under the auspices of the
UNITARIAN UNIVERSALIST ASSOCIATION of CONGREGATIONS.

07 06 05   8 7 6

This book is printed on acid-free paper that meets the uncoated paper ANSI/NISO
specifications for permanence as revised in 1992.

Text design by Isaac Tobin
Composition by Wilsted & Taylor Publishing Services

Library of Congress Cataloging-in-Publication Data

Many children left behind : how the No Child Left Behind Act is
damaging our children and our schools / edited by Deborah Meier
and George Wood.— 1st pbk. ed.
      p. cm.
   Includes bibliographical references.
   ISBN 0-8070-0459-6 (pbk. : alk. paper)
      1. United States. No Child Left Behind Act of 2001. 2. Educational
accountability—Law and legislation—United States. 3. Education—
United States—Evaluation. 4. Educational equalization—United States.
I. Meier, Deborah. II. Wood, George H. (George Harrison)

LB2806.22.M36 2004
379.2'6'0973—dc22   2004006385

Contents

Introduction

GEORGE WOOD

Who could object to a law that promises no child left behind when it comes to our schools? After all, isn't this the great promise of our public school system—that all children, regardless of race, socioeconomic status, gender, creed, color, or disability will have equal access to an education that allows them to enjoy the freedoms and exercise the responsibilities of citizenship in our democracy?

As proposed, the federal No Child Left Behind (NCLB) legislation stood as a continuation of this historic promise. It is a promise that began with Thomas Jefferson's proposal for the first free system of public education in Virginia; a promise offered as the balance wheel of society by the first state superintendent of education, Horace Mann; a promise put forward as the most basic of human rights by W. E. B. DuBois.

Great strides were made to fulfill this promise in the second half of the twentieth century in terms of access. The landmark Supreme Court decision, *Brown v. Board of Education*, which celebrated its fiftieth anniversary in May of 2004 led this push, insisting that all children, regardless of color, should go to school together in order to ensure equality. For young women the landmark was the Title 9 legislation. And for children with handicaps and learning disabilities, the Education for All Handicapped Children Act in 1975 shoved open the schoolhouse doors to full and free access. It is a hard-won tradition of which America should be proud.

But beyond access there was a growing concern with the quality of the school experience for every child. As Ted Sizer points out in his "Preamble" to this volume, the forerunner of NCLB was the landmark Elementary and Secondary Education Act (ESEA) of 1965. For the first time as a nation we acknowledged that access alone was not enough. Rather, some children, given the condition of their childhood, would require more help if *access* to schooling was to be translated into *success* at school. ESEA and its multiple titles (Title 1 reading programs, for example) targeted dollars to communities with the greatest need. ESEA, together with Head Start, also established in 1965, staked out the earliest claims that the achievement gap between rich and poor students could be closed in schools with the right support and interventions.

As we learned four decades later it has not been an easy job. Today, children of color and children of the poor still do not fare as well in school as their wealthier, white counterparts. Of course, this should come as no surprise to us when, as Stan Karp points out in his essay in this book, we only attempt to change one part of the equation for these groups. While efforts have been focused on school improvement, almost nothing has changed during these years for the poor or minorities in terms of a host of other gaps—from health care to housing.

And yet, our faith in public schools as the great equalizer remains, and frustration with our failures led to the most recent attempt to live up to our democratic aspirations—No Child Left Behind.

It is important to remember that NCLB, the 2002 reauthorization of ESEA, was born in bipartisan spirit to do something positive in the wake of the terrorist attacks of September 11,

2001. As the nation continued to rediscover its footing the time seemed right to do something together for our children. Motives are hard to decipher. As Alfie Kohn's essay points out, NCLB was a Trojan horse for those who would challenge the very notion of a public school system. A tool not to strengthen our schools but a ticking time bomb set to destroy them as the punitive sanctions of the law kicked in.

But other proponents of NCLB undoubtedly felt they were doing the right thing for our children and our public schools. The right thing included increasing funding for schools that serve the poor; ensuring that every child would be taught by highly qualified teachers; and holding schools that take federal funds accountable for raising achievement of every student by "disaggregating" their achievement data. The last of these new mandates was, for many, the most important. No longer would school districts be able to disguise the failure of those the federal funds were meant to target (children of color, the poor, and the handicapped), since the achievement scores of those children would be sorted out and reported separately.

Of course, as with most federal legislation, the nearly 1,000-page bill included plenty of special interest pleading and ideological agendas. For example, schools are now mandated to turn over student contact information to the military for recruiting purposes. The Department of Education must certify Title 1 reading programs as "scientifically based"; districts must certify that no policy prevents the participation in "constitutionally protected prayer in public schools"; and no district or school can prohibit the Boy Scouts or any other group listed as a "patriotic society" under U. S. code access to school facilities. But the most ideologically and politically charged tactic—the inclusion of school vouchers to be used for private school attendance—was pulled by the White

House from the legislation in order to maintain a bipartisan spirit to the law.

With this background, why is it that only two years later educators, legislators, and even entire states are in open revolt over NCLB? One does not have to look further than the daily papers to see the news. In Utah and Virginia the legislative bodies have voted nearly unanimously not to comply with NCLB. The roll call of states rejecting some or all of NCLB's provisions includes Hawaii, Arizona, New Mexico, and Vermont. New Hampshire's tack was to reduce state funding for standardized testing to just $1. The nation's largest teachers' union has come out four-square against the legislation, this time joined by administrators in the form of anti-NCLB resolutions passed by the Connecticut Association of Public School Superintendents, the Illinois Association of School Administrators, and Montana South Central Administrators, among many others. Opinion polls show that while parents want their schools to be accountable, the more they know about NCLB the more they oppose it. For the first time in recent memory a single piece of educational legislation has landed front and center in the campaign for the presidency of the United States.

Most of these concerns have been expressed over technical issues with NCLB, and most certainly these should be addressed. Among those immediate concerns are the following:

UNDERFUNDING. *By some estimates the current requests for funding NLCB from the administration fall as much as $12 billion short of the requirements of the legislation. William Mathis, a superintendent in Vermont and professor of educational finance found in his review of state assessments of NCLB costs that on average the funding would have to be increased by 28 percent per state in order to be adequate.*

RESTRICTIVE DEFINITIONS OF TEACHER QUALIFICATIONS. *Many lawmakers in states with large rural populations are finding that the mandates on teacher quality, which focus almost solely on subject matter expertise, make it impossible to hire teachers in some subject areas for schools that need teachers who can teach in multiple areas.*

EFFECTS ON SUBGROUPS. *Demands that disabled and limited English proficient students reach proficiency set those students and their teachers up for failure. Clearly some students simply cannot pass the tests required to demonstrate proficiency and yet no provision is made for alternatives.*

The premise of this book is that *even if these technical problems are fixed, NCLB cannot, will not, and perhaps was even not intended to deliver on its promises.*

Americans were promised that as a result of the targets, incentives, and punishments associated with NCLB we would have higher-quality, more equitable, and more accountable public schools. All of these are laudable goals. And many of those who supported NCLB believed that this legislation would finally fulfill our promises to educate all children. By placing high-quality teachers in schools and identifying 2014 as a target date for every child to be competent as measured by standardized tests, quality schools would be mandated. Focusing on hidden failures in districts by disaggregating data would no longer allow districts to claim unwarranted success, and something would actually be done about the inequality of school outcomes. Schools would be accountable to their communities on a wide range of publicly accessible measures. Quality, equity, community, the cornerstones of a strong public school system, were promised to all by NCLB.

The problem is that regardless of the tinkering around the

edges that may go on with NCLB, it simply cannot deliver the goods.

Start with school quality. NCLB is premised on the notion that schools will be made better by following a yearly testing regime that leads to every child being proficient in reading, math, and science by 2014. The problem is that by limiting all school success measures to one test score *the quality of schools will actually decline.* We continue to confuse test scores with quality schooling, even thought there is no evidence that high scores on these tests predict anything about a child's success in life after school. Drawing on our experiences working in schools and researching school change, the pieces in this book by Linda Darling-Hammond and myself illustrate what happens when one measure of school quality, a standardized test, is used. Simply put, with a focus on testing the curriculum is narrowed, leading to the most ineffective teaching practices becoming the norm. As non-tested areas (art, music, social studies) and "frills" (field trips, naps, even recess) are eliminated, the school experience becomes limited, and everyone—children, parents, and communities—reports less satisfaction with the school.

To make matters worse, these effects of the reliance on one test are disproportionately felt in schools that serve the poor. Drawing from our experience in the field it seems clear that *under NCLB the children of the poor will receive even more limited instruction, curriculum, and school experiences because their schools will be the first to be reported in need of improvement.* Schools that serve affluent populations will continue to find ways to fine-tune their work to move test scores up, with some of that fine-tuning coming in the form of pushing out students who are not expected to test well. Further exacerbating this problem for schools that serve the poor are the NCLB sanctions if a school does not succeed in meeting competency targets. These include having to pay to bus students who choose to transfer to another school, mandated funding of after-school tutoring, and similar unproven strategies that will stretch already limited resources even thinner. It is a cruel irony that legislation designed to help the poorest of schools and students will hurt those schools and children the most.

Finally, *NCLB will make public schools even less accountable to the publics they serve.* Much has been said about accountability in the debates about our schools, but little of the rhetoric has been focused on those our schools are accountable to. Historically, we have relied on a system of local accountability and local trust. Schools are primarily funded by local taxes, run by a local school board, and serve local children who are taught by those who live among them. As Deborah Meier points out in her essay, this local bond has been steadily eroded, undercutting much support for our schools. NCLB with its mandates will only further extend this erosion of public trust and control as schools are first forced to meet testing standards set by state bureaucrats and, if they fail to meet standards, are ultimately taken over and run from the state capital.

What is to be done? If NCLB cannot deliver on its promises but they are promises nonetheless that Americans want kept, what alternatives are there? In several of the essays here the author suggests other ways to improve our schools, because opposing NCLB is not to oppose school reform. In fact, every one of the individuals who volunteered their time and expertise for this book project work daily as teachers, administrators, consultants, policy makers, or in other roles working for better schools. None of us needed another series of tests to show us that our schools, especially those serving the most vulnerable of our children, need improvement. For us, opposing NCLB is not about "turning back the clock" or succumbing to a "tyranny of low expectations," as some politicians accuse those who raise questions about NCLB of doing. Rather, it is about, as Stan Karp puts it, transforming NCLB from a "test-and-punish law to a school improvement law."

Monty Neill's piece concludes this book and sets forth an outline of how that transformation could occur. He begins with a look at principles that should guide genuine accountability and moves on to the real work of how to support and assess schools. Additionally, in several of the other essays here proposals are offered for ways to support schools and teachers who are working to make a difference for our kids in the most difficult of conditions. In each case the recommendations are based on an awareness that schools cannot do this alone and that more targeted resources for the needs of the growing number of poor children in our country must be forthcoming if, as the slogan of the Children's Defense Fund says, we are to "leave no child behind." But these proposals also point out the things schools can do, which, based on the authors' experiences, do work for all of our children.

Together the essays in this book demonstrate the counterproductive and destructive effects of NCLB. They also provide us with an agenda for change. An agenda that builds on a growing public dissatisfaction with a law that mandates a one-size-fits-all testing program, unfairly judges schools based on those tests, hurts quality school programs, unequally impacts children, hinders the professional judgment of our teachers, and limits the accountability schools have to those they serve—parents and their children. It is an agenda that focuses attention on how good schools came to be, not through testing mandates but through sensitivity to local communities and their needs. An agenda that includes smaller schools where children are better known; high standards of demonstrated achievement, not just test scores; well-prepared, well-supported, and well-paid teachers; clean, safe, and well-supplied schoolhouses; community and parent input into school goals; and equitable school resources for every child.

This is an agenda that takes the intent of "no child left behind" from a slogan to reality. An agenda that pulls together the civil rights organizations that applaud no longer hiding our schools' failure to educate poor and minority children, the educators who work for school reform, the parents and civic groups that want better schools, and the legislators who work hard for what is best for their constituents. A movement that springs not from mandates and measurement, punishment and penalties, sanctions and closures, but rather, a movement that grows from hope and wisdom—hope that we can have the public schools our democracy requires, based on the wisdom that we have gained from schools that serve our children well regardless of race, class, gender, handicaps, or geography.

The authors of this book aim to add to this movement, as they agree with the premise that no child should be left behind, yet recognize that in NCLB many children will not only be left behind, but will be damaged as well—in ways we are just now beginning to understand.

Preamble: A Reminder for Americans

THEODORE R. SIZER

The measure of the worth of a society is how it treats its weakest and most vulnerable citizens.

By this standard, America—the richest nation in the history of the world—falls visibly short. We are long on rhetoric and short on resolute action. The gap between our articulated ideals and our practice is an international embarrassment.

It does not have to be so. Government in a responsible democracy has the tools to narrow the gap between our ideals and our actions. Accomplishing this narrowing, however, will not be easy. We are short on the habit of seeing our community as a *commonwealth,* one which at once honors individual's entrepreneurial energy, protects our private lives, and provides the means for those who are weak today to be secure and productive tomorrow. Those of us who are secure in life have too often been loath to put our secure condition at any risk by sharing with those who are insecure.

In a healthy democracy, however, principled politics are the means equitably and wisely to address this difficult task—one of remembering our democratic duties and acting upon them—as soon as possible.

Free public schooling has long been the primary engine for social and economic health and for individual social mobility. America's economic, social, and moral strength still depends on it. As the culture changes, the shape of "public education" should change with it, but in a way that always keeps the *public* in "public education" secure.

Americans, and especially their elected leaders, do well to ponder the principles of a truly public education in a free society. Some of these are venerable, icons of this nation. Most are obvious:

The People will provide for thorough and efficient schooling for all children.

The People will tax themselves for this purpose.

While education is to be the constitutional responsibility of each of the states, the schools will remain close to the citizens served. *Ours never was to be either a national system or a centrally directed state system, with a few exceptions, largely due to geography.*

All citizens will have access to these schools. *Since their inception, they were* public; *up to a certain age young citizens were required to attend; and the People, close to those young citizens particularly served, would, with certain exceptions, govern the shape of their local schools.*

The schools' professionals would be "trained" privately in autonomous teacher education institutions (public and private), hired locally, and certified at the state level.

Most of these conditions emerged when America's population was small. Paradoxically, as the nation grew, authority gradually moved upward to the federal level, usually when state and local communities had so egregiously abused these principles that national constitutional remedies were required. Well-known examples are *Brown v. Board of Education of Topeka, Kansas,* in 1954, on the matter of access limited by race; the Elementary and Secondary Education Act of 1965, on the matter of discrimination by economic class; and the Education for All Handicapped Children Act in 1975, on the matter of inadequate services provided for children with special needs.

What is today emerging is a new balance between governmental levels, federal, state, and local. A rebalancing may be necessary, but the need to redistribute some governmental responsibility in education should not trump the traditional principles of public education articulated above.

Emerging today are trends that threaten the historic promise of public education and we need to address them:

- *Inadequately funded or equipped schools, however efficient, rarely provide a thorough education.*

- *In poor communities, local taxation cannot support minimally acceptable schooling. State and federal equalization formulas rarely cover the cost differences between poor districts and wealthy districts.*

- *Argued on the basis of local incompetence, state and federal detailed direction of school routines has abruptly grown over the last decade.*

- *In most states, access to public education is limited by one's neighborhood. The effect is that wealthier families have access to schools with more robust funding than do their poorer neighbors. Segregation by social class is the rule, not the exception.*

• *Again argued on the basis of incompetence, the authority of teachers and principals has increasingly been narrowed.*

These trends deserve vigorous challenge. Ironically, the major piece of recent relevant federal legislation, the so-called No Child Left Behind Act (NCLB), takes us in the opposite direction from the one in which we need to move.

The sad irony is that NCLB is, in fact, primarily the most recent reauthorization of the historic Elementary and Secondary Education Act of 1965 (ESEA, Public Law 89–10), "An Act to strengthen and improve educational quality and educational opportunities in the Nation's elementary and secondary schools." At that time, some forty years ago, the U.S. Office of Education summarized Title I, the central part of the act: "The Office of Education would allocate the money to state educational agencies, which have full responsibility to see that the purposes of the Act are carried out.... Each local education agency must come up with its own plan for upgrading the education of deprived children.... Needs and requirements would vary from State to State and district to district. The type of programs that would best meet these needs and requirements would be left to the discretion and judgment of the State and local educational agencies.... The new legislation encourages local school districts to use imaginative thinking and new approaches."[1]

NCLB radically centralizes, by means of federal approval of state plans, one key element of school operation—the definition of "standards" in several key areas and the ways and means of assessing them. Members of the 89th Congress in 1965, especially its Republicans, would have had heart failure if presented with this current reauthorization of ESEA and the way it places substantial power and direction in the hands of the federal government. The penalties imposed on districts that "underperform" on the basis of the NCLB are specific and standardized. By contrast, the 89th Congress wanted detailed decisions about educational matters left unequivocally in state and local hands. Wisdom was never especially felt to reside in Washington.

NCLB reflects most citizens' justified impatience with the efforts of some states and school districts in addressing the needs of "disadvantaged" children, but the remedies it imposes are ultimately driven by a single kind of instrument, the standardized test. The educational need is defined as a narrowing of the (test score) gap between rich and poor students. While worthy standardized tests do provide teachers with much good data, they hardly provide either enough information or the balance of information necessary to assess accurately either a student's mastery or a district's or school's effort. NCLB narrows, and thus profoundly distorts, the problem.

NCLB ignores many of the reasons for schools' and children's failures, thus leaving the financing of these to state and local governments. The 89th and succeeding Congresses provided federal money and incentives for research, training, and recruitment of teachers and administrators. The current Congress exhibits little, save rhetorical interest in teacher training and development.

While NCLB was accompanied by much rhetorical emphasis on "research-based" education policy, the breath of this research is narrow, largely settled on specific pedagogies and curricula that are "measurable." Compelling research on larger themes—the social reasons for school dropouts, the weakness of social capital in regions with apparently "low-performing" schools, the misdesign of many schools, the evidence of growing inequities among population groups and communities, the impact of now ubiquitous media on the basic learning of children and adolescents, for example—find no place in the act. By contrast, the Congresses of the late

1960s supported major independent research initiatives, most famously the massive, controversial and still provocative "Equal Educational Opportunity Study," led by Professor James S. Coleman.

NCLB places, without remuneration, financially and bureaucratically onerous reporting duties on states, districts, and schools. By contrast, Title V of ESEA of the 89th Congress in 1965 added funds directly to assist state departments of education to carry out and extend the purposes of the Act.

Of course, 2004 is not 1965. And, of course, thoughtful Americans are no less concerned today than forty years ago about the failure of many of our schools to provide for their students a powerful and relevant education. The inequities, all of our making, are a public embarrassment in a serious democracy.

And so we agree on most of the ends. Where we disagree is on many of the means, including many of those embedded in NCLB. Some of us believe that these not only dodge today's major problems of educational excellence and democratic fairness, but, perversely, make them worse.

Thus are this book's stark arguments. No Child Left Behind is its immediate target, but beyond is a larger and positive vision, the creation of a truly fair and powerful system of public schools in America. We argue here not only to make an immediate point about one misdirected act, but to keep alive an educational debate that can lead us toward a system of schooling which is worthy of Americans and the democracy of which its people for generations have dreamed.

PART ONE

NCLB's Effects on
Classrooms and Schools

1: From "Separate but Equal" to "No Child Left Behind": The Collision of New Standards and Old Inequalities

LINDA DARLING-HAMMOND

Many civil rights advocates initially hailed the Bush administration's major education bill, optimistically entitled No Child Left Behind, as a step forward in the long battle to improve education for those children traditionally left behind in American schools—in particular, students of color and students living in poverty, new English learners, and students with disabilities. The broad goal of NCLB is to raise the achievement levels of all students, especially underperforming groups, and to close the achievement gap that parallels race and class distinctions. According to the legislation, too many of the neediest children are being left behind; too many are attending failing or unsafe schools; too many receive poor teaching and are performing well below potential; and too many are leaving school altogether. The bill intends to change this by focusing schools' attention on improving test scores for all groups of students, providing parents with more educational choices, and ensuring better-qualified teachers.

This noble agenda seems unobjectionable on its face, but the complex 600-page law has affected states, districts, schools, and students in ways never envisioned by its authors.

The proliferating nicknames emerging as this intrusive legislation plays out across the country give a sense of some of the anger, bewilderment, and confusion left in its wake: "No Child Left Untested," "No School Board Left Standing," and "No Child's Behind Left" are just a few of them. Since the start of the 2003–04 school year, at least twenty states and a number of school districts have officially protested the NCLB Act, voting to withdraw from participation, to withhold local funding for implementation, or to resist specific provisions. Members of the Congressional Black Caucus, among other federal legislators, have introduced bills to amend the law by placing a moratorium on high-stakes standardized testing, a key element of NCLB; withholding school sanctions until the bill is fully funded; and requiring progress toward adequate and equitable educational opportunities for students in public schools. The Harvard Civil Rights Project, along with other advocacy groups, has warned that the law threatens to increase the growing dropout and pushout rates for students of color, ultimately reducing access to education for these students, rather than enhancing it.[1] As the evidence of NCLB's unintended consequences emerges, it seems increasingly clear that, despite its good intentions and admirable goals, NCLB as currently implemented is more likely to harm than to help most of the students who are the targets of its aspirations, and it is more likely to undermine—some would even say destroy—the nation's public education system than to improve it. These outcomes are likely because the underfunded bill layers onto a grossly unequal—and, in many communities, inadequately funded—school system a set of unmeetable test score targets that disproportionately penalize schools serving the neediest students, while creating strong incentives for schools to keep out or push out those students who are low achieving in order to raise school average test scores.

Furthermore, the act's regulations have caused a number

of states to abandon their thoughtful diagnostic assessment and accountability systems—replacing instructionally rich, improvement-oriented systems with more rote-oriented punishment-driven approaches—and it has thrown many high-performing and steadily improving schools into chaos rather than helping them remain focused and deliberate in their ongoing efforts to serve students well.

While well intentioned, it has become clear that the NCLB Act will, in the next few years, label most of the nation's public schools "failing," even when they are high performing and improving in achievement. According to one tally, 26,000 of the nation's 93,000 public schools this year "failed to make adequate yearly process." A new study in California found that failing "schools were designated not because tests had shown their overall achievement levels to be faltering, but because a single student group—disabled learners or Asian students, for example—had fallen short of a target. As a result, the chances that a school would be designated as failing increased in proportion to the number of demographic groups served by the school."[2] And in some high-achieving states that have set very high standards for themselves, large numbers of schools are dubbed 'failing' because they fall below these standards, even though they score well above most other schools in the nation and the world.

Some believe this is a prelude to voucher proposals aimed at privatizing the education system, since the public will have been besieged with annual reports about failing public schools which the law's unmeetable requirements guarantee cannot be remedied. In addition to the perverse consequences for school systems, the law will lead to reductions in federal funding to already underresourced schools and it will sidetrack funds needed for improvement to underwrite transfers for students to other schools (which, if they are available, may offer no higher quality education). If left unchanged, the act will deflect needed resources for teaching and learning to ever more intensive testing of students, ranking of schools, busing of students, and lawyers' fees for litigating the many unintended consequences of the legislation.

Most unhappily, some of the act's most important and potentially productive components—such as the effort to ensure that all students have highly qualified teachers and successful educational options and supports—are in danger of being extinguished by the shortcomings of a shortsighted, one-way accountability system that holds children and educators to test-based standards they are not enabled to meet, while it does *not* hold federal or state governments to standards that would ensure equal and adequate educational opportunity.

Inequality in Education: What NCLB Does Not Change

The first problem—one that NCLB does not acknowledge or effectively address—is the enormous inequality in the provision of education offered in the United States. Unlike most countries that fund schools centrally and equally, the wealthiest U.S. public schools spend at least ten times more than the poorest schools—ranging from over $30,000 per pupil at the wealthy schools to only $3,000 at the poorest. These disparities contribute to a wider achievement gap in this country than in virtually any other industrialized country in the world. The school disparities documented in Jonathan Kozol's *Savage Inequalities* (1991) have not lessened in recent years. Within states, the spending ratio between high- and low-spending schools is typically at least 3 or 4 to 1.

As documented in federal statistics and a large number of current lawsuits, schools serving large numbers of low-income students and students of color have larger class sizes, fewer teachers and counselors, fewer and lower-quality academic courses, extracurricular activities, books, materials, supplies, and computers, libraries, and special services.[3] Spending is so severely inadequate in the growing number of "apartheid" schools serving more than 90 percent "minority" students that legal action to challenge school funding systems is under way in nearly half the states. These conditions are vividly illustrated in this description of Luther Burbank Middle School, which serves the low-income students of color in San Francisco who are plaintiffs in *Williams v. California*, an equal educational opportunity lawsuit:

At Luther Burbank School, students cannot take textbooks home for homework in any core subject because their teachers have enough textbooks for use in class only.... Some math, science, and other core classes do not have even enough textbooks for all the students in a single class to use during the school day, so some students must share the same one book during class time.... For homework, students must take home photocopied pages, with no accompanying text for guidance or reference, when and if their teachers have enough paper to use to make homework copies.... The social studies textbook Luther Burbank students use is so old that it does not reflect the breakup of the former Soviet Union. Luther Burbank is infested with vermin and roaches and students routinely see mice in their classrooms. One dead rodent has remained, decomposing, in a corner in the gymnasium since the beginning of the school year. The school library is rarely open, has no librarian, and has not recently been updated. Luther Burbank classrooms do not have computers. Computer instruction and research skills are not, therefore, part of Luther Burbank students' regular instruction in their core courses. The school no longer offers any art classes for budgetary reasons. Two of the three bathrooms at Luther Burbank are locked all day, every day. The third bathroom is locked during lunch and other periods during the school day, so there are times during school when no bathroom at all is available for students

> to use. *Students have urinated or defecated on themselves at school because they could not get into an unlocked bathroom. . . . When the bathrooms are not locked, they often lack toilet paper, soap, and paper towels, and the toilets frequently are clogged and overflowing. . . . Ceiling tiles are missing and cracked in the school gym, and school children are afraid to play basketball and other games in the gym because they worry that more ceiling tiles will fall on them during their games. . . . The school heating system does not work well. In winter, children often wear coats, hats, and gloves during class to keep warm. Eleven of the 35 teachers at Luther Burbank have not yet obtained regular, non-emergency credentials, and 17 of the 35 teachers only began teaching at Luther Burbank this school year.* (Williams v. State of California, *Superior Court of the State of CA for the County of San Francisco, 2001, Complaint 58–66*).

It should be no surprise that the students at Luther Burbank and schools like it achieve at low levels and often fail state-imposed tests, ending their school careers with less opportunity to play a productive role in society than when they began as eager kindergartners.

Under No Child Left Behind, these dreadful school conditions are left largely untouched. Although the act orders schools to ensure that 100 percent of students test at levels identified as "proficient" by the year 2014—and to make mandated progress toward this goal each year—the small per pupil dollar allocation it makes to schools serving low-income students is well under 10 percent of schools' total spending, far too little to correct these conditions. Most of the federal money has to be spent for purposes other than upgraded facilities, textbooks, or teachers' salaries. Furthermore, while the law focuses on test scores as indicators of school quality, it largely ignores the important inputs or resources that *enable* school quality. It does not authorize substantial federal investments in the underresourced schools where many students are currently struggling to learn, nor does it require that states demonstrate progress toward equitable and adequate funding or greater "opportunities to learn." Although the law includes another set of requirements to ensure that all students receive "highly qualified teachers," as discussed in a later section, the lack of adequate federal support for actually making this possible currently appears to make this promise a rather hollow one in many communities.

To Test or to Invest? How NCLB Treats Schools
Serving the Nation's Neediest Students

The biggest problem with the NCLB Act is that it mistakes measuring schools for fixing them. It sets annual test score goals for every school—and for subgroups of students within schools—that are said to constitute "Adequate Yearly Progress." Schools that do not meet these targets for each subgroup each year are declared in need of improvement and, later, failing. This triggers interventions (notification to parents of the school's label and a three-month period to write a school improvement plan). Students must be allowed to transfer out of "failing" schools at the school's expense, schools stand to be reconstituted or closed, and states and districts stand to lose funds based on these designations. Unfortunately, the targets—based on the notion that 100 percent of students will score at the "proficient" level on state tests by the year 2014—were set without an understanding of what this goal would really mean.

First, of course, there is the fundamental problem that it is impossible to attain 100 percent proficiency levels for students on norm-referenced tests (when 50 percent of students by definition must score below the norm and some proportion must by definition score below any cut point selected), which are the kind of tests that have been adopted by an increasing number of states due to the specific annual testing requirements of NCLB. Criterion-referenced tests also typically use an underlying norm-referenced logic in selecting items and setting cut scores, although in theory, the target could at least remain fixed on these tests. Even if tests were not constructed in this way, the steepness of the standard is unrealistic. Using a definition of proficiency benchmarked to the National Assessment of Educational Progress (NAEP), one analyst has calculated that it would take schools more than one hundred years to reach such a target in all content areas if they continued the fairly brisk rate of progress they were making during the 1990s.[4]

Even more problematic is that the act requires that schools be declared "failing" if they fail to meet these targets for each subgroup of designated students annually. It requires the largest gains from lower-performing schools, ignoring that these schools serve needier students and are generally less well funded than those serving wealthier and higher-scoring students. To complicate things more, those that serve large numbers of new English language learners (what the law calls Limited English Proficient [LEP] students) and some kinds of special needs students (what the law calls "students with disabilities") are further penalized by the fact that students are assigned to these subgroups *because* they cannot meet the standard, and they are typically removed from the subgroup when they do meet the standard. Thus these schools will not ever be able to meet the annual AYP (adequate yearly progress standard), which demands that schools advance yearly to 100 percent student proficiency.

For example, section 9101(25) of NCLB defines an LEP student as one "(D) whose difficulties in speaking, reading, writing, or understanding the English language may be sufficient to deny the individual—(i) *the ability to meet the State's proficient level of achievement* on State assessments described in section 1111(b)(3)." As students gain proficiency in English, they are transferred out of this subgroup; thus, it is impossible for 100 percent of this subgroup ever to reach proficiency. For schools and districts that serve a substantial number of LEP students, this imposes a ceiling on their overall performance as well as the performance of this subgroup. At some point it will be impossible to make the required gains because of how this subgroup is defined under law. Some advocates have suggested that states use a rule that scores of students who are classified as LEP should be counted in the AYP calculations for this subgroup as long as they stay in a school. However, the U.S. Department of Education has not approved this definition.[5]

The same issues pertain to the testing of students with disabilities and to the schools that serve them. Many such students who cannot demonstrate their learning on grade-level tests have individualized education plans that prescribe different assessments for charting their progress, including "instructional level" tests. The Department of Education has ruled that using such tests is permissible only if the results are counted as "nonproficient," or—for one year only—if they apply to fewer than 1 percent of all test-takers. In addition to appearing to violate special education laws, schools that serve large numbers of special education students will be penalized in their AYP rankings. Because disabilities are correlated with poverty (which is linked to poor prenatal and childhood health care, low birth weight, poor nutrition, lead poisoning, maternal substance abuse, and many other conditions that predict learning problems), this is yet another way in which NCLB punishes schools and districts that serve large numbers of low-income students.

For all of these reasons, two separate teams of researchers have found that, in the early years of NCLB implementation, schools serving poor, minority, and LEP students and those with a greater number of subgroups for which they are held accountable are disproportionately identified as "needing improvement"—what one group of researchers has called a "diversity penalty."[6] As illustrated below, this is true even for schools that show steep test score gains for low-income and minority students.

For example, Novak and Fuller identified two schools in Oakland whose students, on average, performed at equal levels on standardized tests. One, Manzanita Elementary, serves a diverse population, including black, Latino, Asian, low-income and limited-English students. The other school, Golden Gate Elementary, serves primarily black students, some of whom are also in the low-income category, giving the school just two groups under the federal law's accountability system. As a result of its diverse population, Manzanita had to meet targets in eighteen categories—each of these subgroups on several different content tests. It succeeded in seventeen, but black students narrowly missed their target in math. Golden Gate, because of its more homogeneous student body, needed to meet targets in only six categories, and succeeded. Manzanita was designated as needing improvement, and Golden Gate was not. Among the most diverse districts in California—Fresno, Los Angeles, Oakland, San Francisco, San Jose, and Santa Ana—half or more of all schools failed to meet all of their AYP growth targets in 2003, thus positioning these districts serving the state's neediest students for large reductions in federal funding within a short period of time.

While these are troubling aspects of the law's implementation, one could also argue, quite legitimately, that many of the schools identified as "needing improvement" (a designation that changes to "failing" if not corrected after three years) indeed are dismal places where little learning occurs, or are complacent schools that have not attended to the needs of all of their students—schools that need to be jolted into action to change. It is fair to suggest that students in such schools deserve other choices if they cannot change.

These important arguments are part of the NCLB's theory of action: that low-quality schools will be motivated to change if they are identified and shamed, and that their students will be better served if given other educational options. These outcomes may in fact occur in some cases. The problem is that the law actually works in many other cases to label schools as failing even when they are succeeding with the very students the law wants to help, and it creates incentives that can reduce the quality of education such schools can provide, while providing few real options for their students to go to better schools.

How might the goal of improving schools actually, paradoxically, undermine them? First, there is evidence from states that have used similar accountability provisions that applying labels of failure to low-scoring schools that serve low-income students reduces the schools' ability to attract and keep qualified teachers. For example, in North Carolina, analysts found that the state labeling system made it more difficult for the neediest schools to get access to the higher-quality teachers other state policies were attracting and developing in the state.[7] Similarly, Florida's use of aggregate test scores, unadjusted for student characteristics, to allocate school rewards and sanctions led to reports that qualified teachers were leaving the schools rated D or F in droves, to be replaced by teachers without experience or training.[8] As one principal queried, "Is anybody going to want to dedicate their lives to a school that has already been labeled a failure?" NCLB's requirements for parent notification of school "needs improvement" or "failing" label and threats of staff dismissal have already been reported as disincentives for qualified staff to stay in high-need schools when they have options to teach in better resourced and better regarded schools with more affluent students.

Second, schools that have been identified as not meeting AYP standards stand to lose federal funding, thus having even fewer resources to spend on the students they are serving. Rather than seeking to ensure that students attend adequately funded and well-managed schools that would enable them to learn to higher levels, NCLB seeks to expand students' opportunities by offering them the chance to transfer out to other "non-failing" public schools if their school is declared "failing." This option is to be funded through the resources of the "failing" school, as are funds for supplemental services for such things as tutoring or after-school programs.

While the choice option is a useful idea in theory, such alternatives are likely to reap little overall improvement in the opportunities for most students in poor rural or inner-city schools, because—in addition to the fact that this option for some comes at the expense of school funding for their peers—there are frequently no "non-failing" public schools with open seats available to transfer to nearby. The best schools are already quite full, and these schools have no incentive to admit low-income students with low test scores, poor attendance records, or substantial educational needs who will "bring down" their average and place the school at risk of receiving sanctions. Furthermore, the best-resourced schools are typically not close to the inner city or poor rural neighborhoods where struggling schools are concentrated. Thus, rather than expanding educational opportunities for low-income students and students of color, the law is more likely in many communities to reduce still further the quality of education available in the schools they must attend. A better approach would be to invest in the needed improvements in such schools in the first place, and to measure their progress on a variety of indicators in ways that give the schools credit for improvements they produce for the students they serve.

"Alice in Wonderland" Accountability

The goals of No Child Left Behind are to improve achievement for all students, to enhance equity, and to ensure more qualified teachers. However, its complex regulations for showing "Adequate Yearly Progress" toward test score targets aimed at "100% proficiency" within ten years have created a bizarre situation in which most of the nation's public schools will be deemed failing within the next few years—even many that already score high and those that are steadily improving from year to year. Ironically, states that use more ambitious tests and have set higher standards will experience greater failures than those with low standards, and many have abandoned measures of critical thinking and performance, just as the labor market increasingly demands these kinds of skills. Here are a few examples of the strange and curious outcomes of the law thus far:

In San Diego, Marston Middle School, a well-regarded school serving a diverse student population with a large number of low-income, minority, and English-language-learning students, has been showing large gains in achievement for all groups each year as its dedicated principal and teachers have worked intensely on school-wide literacy development.[9] The school once again saw huge gains in 2003, far exceeding its growth target and showing gains for Latino students and low-income students of more than four times the targeted increases. This caused the school's achievement gap to shrink substantially. However, under NCLB the school was declared in "need of improvement," because its white students, who already score near the top of the state accountability index, did not improve "sufficiently"—largely because they have hit the testing ceiling, and, as a group, have little room for further growth. Marston Middle School is doing what NCLB intended schools to do—increase achievement and reduce the achievement gap—but it will be punished under the law, and its students will lose funds that could have gone to support their education and the ongoing improvement of the school.

Meanwhile, in Minnesota, where, as Garrison Keillor claims, "all of the women are pretty and all of the children are above average," eighth graders score first in the nation in mathematics and near the top in other subjects as well. However, a recent news report notes that, under the rules of No Child Left Behind, more than 80 percent of Minnesota's public schools will soon be declared "in need of improvement," and not long after, if they don't meet the law's targets for "Adequate Yearly Progress," declared as "failing" and in need of reconstitution. This is because, in the baffling world that has become federal policy, schools in states with the highest standards will have the most schools found wanting, even if their students achieve at levels substantially above those of schools in other states.

One of the first perverse consequences of the NCLB Act is that many states formally lowered their standards in order to avoid having most of their schools declared failing. Another perverse consequence is that states that have worked hard to create forward-looking assessment systems during the 1990s have begun to abandon them, since they do not fit the federal mandate for annual testing that allows students and schools to be ranked and compared. In fact, NCLB is undoing some of the most important gains in assessment and accountability made by states since 1990, when the Goals 2000 Act encouraged them to create such systems. In the past decade, virtually all states have created new standards that reflect what students should know and be able to do, new curriculum frameworks to guide instruction, and new assessments to test students' knowledge. Advocates of these reforms have hoped that setting standards would mobilize resources for student learning, including high-quality curriculum, materials, and assessments tied to the standards; more widely available course offerings that reflect this high-quality curriculum; more intensive teacher preparation guided by related standards for teaching; more equal resources for schools; and more readily available safety nets for educationally needy students.

This comprehensive approach has been followed in some states and districts, including Connecticut, Kentucky, Maine, Maryland, Minnesota, Nebraska, Vermont, and Washington, among others. In these cases, thoughtful assessments have been tied to investments in improved schooling and teaching. These efforts have begun to improve student achievement while enhancing teaching and increasing educational opportunity. Many of these states created sophisticated assessments that measure critical thinking and real performance in areas like writing, mathematical and scientific problem solving, and research. They developed their systems carefully over a sustained period of time and have used them primarily to inform ongoing school improvement—identifying areas of needed curriculum change, professional development, and additional investments—rather than to punish students or schools.

Much of this effort threatens to be undone by NCLB's requirements for annual tests that meet certain federal specifications. NCLB's test requirements and costs have already caused one state, Maryland, to drop its sophisticated performance assessment system and another, Vermont, to threaten to reject the new federal funds in order to maintain its performance assessments. Maine eliminated a number of its assessments in fields like social studies and the arts, as well as its teacher scoring process which provided strong professional development. Oregon has fought to get the Department of Education to allow it to use its sophisticated computer-based adaptive testing system for the purposes of both diagnosis for instruction and standards-based assessment it was designed to serve. States like Nebraska that previously used only performance assessments to evaluate student learning have been forced to adopt norm-referenced standardized tests to meet the law's requirements.[10] NCLB regulations are pushing states back to the lowest common denominator in testing, undoing progress that has been made to improve the quality of assessments and delaying the move from antiquated norm-referenced, multiple-choice tests to criterion-referenced assessment systems that measure and help develop important kinds of performance and learning.

This not only reduces the chances that schools will be able to focus on helping students acquire critical thinking, research, writing, and production abilities; it will also reduce opportunities for students who learn in different ways and have different talents to show what they have learned. Analysts have raised many concerns about how the law's requirements are leading to a narrower curriculum; to test-based instruction that ignores critical real world skills, especially for lower-income and lower-performing students; and to less useful and engaging education.[11] These are all important concerns. Equally important is the strong possibility that these efforts will actually reduce access to education for the most vulnerable students, rather than increasing it.

Higher Scores, Fewer Students

Perhaps the most adverse, unintended consequence of NCLB's accountability strategy is that it undermines safety nets for struggling students rather than expanding them. The accountability provisions of the NCLB Act actually create large incentives for other schools to keep such students out and for all schools to hold back or push out students who are not doing well. As low-scoring students disappear, test scores go up. Table 1 shows how this operates. At "King Middle School," average scores increased from the 70th to the 72nd percentile between the 2002 and 2003 school year, and the proportion of students in attendance who met the standard (a score of 65) increased from 66 to 80 percent—the kind of performance that test-based accountability systems, including NCLB, celebrate and reward. Looking at subgroup performance, the proportion of Latino students meeting the standard increased from 33 to 50 percent, a steep increase.

However, *not a single student* at King improved his or her score between 2002 and 2003. In fact, the scores of every single student in the school went *down* over the course of the year. How could these steep improvements in the school's average scores and proficiency rates have occurred? A close look at table 1 shows that the major change between the two years was that the lowest-scoring student, Raul, disappeared. As

TABLE 1: KING MIDDLE SCHOOL: REWARDS OR SANCTIONS?

The Relationship Between Test Score Trends and Student Population

	2002–03	2003–04
Laura	100	90
James	90	80
Felipe	80	70
Kisha	70	65
Jose	60	55
Raul	20	
	Av. Score = 70	Av. Score = 72
	% meeting standard = 66%	% meeting standard = 80%

has occurred in many states with high-stakes testing programs, students who do poorly on the tests—special needs students, new English language learners, those with poor attendance, health, or family problems—are increasingly likely to be excluded by being counseled out, transferred, expelled, or by dropping out.

If this school had been judged using a "value-added" index that looked at the changes in individual students' scores from one year to the next, it would have been clear that the students' scores decreased by 8 percentile points on average rather than registering an apparent, but illusory, gain caused by changes in the student population. Recent studies have found that systems that reward or sanction schools based on average student scores (rather than looking at the growth of individual students) create incentives for pushing low-scorers into special education so that their scores won't count in school reports,[12] retaining students in grade so that their grade-level scores will look better,[13] excluding low-scoring students from admissions,[14] and encouraging such students to leave schools or drop out.[15] Studies have linked dropout rates in Georgia, Florida, Massachusetts, New York, and North Carolina to the effects of grade retention, student discouragement, and school exclusion policies stimulated by high-stakes tests. According to the National Center for Education Statistics, graduation rates decreased from 63 to 58 percent in New York between 1997 and 2001 and from 57 to 52 percent in Florida as new high-stakes testing policies were introduced.

Recent data from Massachusetts, which began to implement high-stakes testing in the late 1990s, show more grade retention and higher dropout rates, including a 300 percent increase in middle school dropouts between 1997–1998 and 1999–2000, greater proportions of students dropping out in ninth and tenth grades, more of them African American and

Latino, and fewer dropouts returning to school. When the state's exit exam was first enforced in 2003, graduation rates for the group of ninth graders who had entered high school four years earlier decreased for all students, but most sharply for students of color. Whereas state data showed a graduation rate of 71 percent for African American students in the class of 2002, the class of 2003 had only 59.5 percent in line to graduate (still in school and having passed the exams in the spring of 2003). The drop for Latino students went from 54 percent in 2002 to 45 percent in 2003, and for Asian students from 89 percent to 81 percent.[16] Meanwhile many of the steepest increases in test scores have occurred in schools with the highest retention and dropout rates. For example, Wheelock found that, in addition to increasing dropout rates, high schools receiving state awards for gains in tenth-grade pass rates on the MCAS (the Massachusetts test) showed substantial increases in prior year ninth-grade retention rates and in the percentage of "missing" tenth graders.[17]

Although the hope is that such carrots and sticks will force schools to improve, this does not necessarily occur. Last year, news reports revealed what researchers had previously observed—that the "Texas Miracle," which was the model for the federal No Child Left Behind Act, boosted test scores in part by keeping many students out of the testing count and making tens of thousands disappear from school altogether.[18] The "disappeared" are mostly students of color. At Sharpstown High School in Houston, a freshman class of 1,000 dwindled to fewer than 300 students by senior year—a pattern seen in most high-minority high schools in Houston, including those rewarded for getting their test scores "up." The miracle is that not one dropout was reported. The whistle-blowing principal from Sharpstown has described how this pattern is widespread and encouraged by the district.[19]

In Texas, where tests alone are supposed to drive improvement, large numbers of students of color are taught by under-prepared and inexperienced teachers—which significantly affects passing rates on the state tests.[20] Fewer than 70 percent of white students who enter ninth grade graduate from high school four years later, and the proportions for African-American and Latino students are under 50 percent.[21] Unhappily, the score gains for African-American and Latino students celebrated in Houston appear in part to be a function of high dropout and push out rates for these students. As low-achievers leave school, the group's average score increases. Paradoxically, NCLB's requirement for disaggregating data and tracking progress for each subgroup of students may increase the incentives for eliminating those at the bottom of each subgroup who struggle to learn, especially where schools have little capacity to improve the quality of services such students receive.

Where states have replaced investing with testing, the sad story in too many cities and poor rural communities is that students are forced to attend underresourced schools where they lack the texts, materials, qualified teachers, computers, and other necessities for learning. In lieu of resources, the state offers tests, which are used to hold students back if they do not reach benchmarks (a practice found to increase later dropout rates but not to improve achievement) and to deny them diplomas, which in today's economy is the equivalent of denying access to the economy and to a productive life. In these states, two-way accountability does not exist. The child is accountable to the state for test performance, but the state is not held accountable to the child for a basic level of education. No Child Left Behind exacerbates this problem by adding to the incentives some states have already created for getting rid of the troublesome youth who don't score high and introducing these incentives to other states in the country.

There is no doubt that the current conditions of schooling

for many students of color and low-income students in the United States strongly resemble those that existed before *Brown v. Board of Education* sought to end separate and unequal education. Unfortunately, this law, though rhetorically appearing to address these problems, actually threatens to leave more children behind. The incentives created by an approach that substitutes high-stakes testing for highly effective teaching are pushing more and more of the most educationally vulnerable students out of school earlier and earlier. In a growing number of states, high school completion rates for African-American and Latino students have returned to pre-1954 levels.

The consequences for individual students who are caught in this no-win situation can be tragic, as most cannot go on to further education or even military service if they fail these tests, drop out, or are pushed out to help their schools' scores look better. The consequences for society are also tragic, as more and more students are leaving school earlier and earlier—some with only a seventh- or eighth-grade education—without the skills to be able to join the economy. These students join what is increasingly known as a "school-to-prison pipeline" carrying an increasing number of undereducated youth almost directly into the criminal justice system. Indeed, prison enrollments have tripled since the 1980s and the costs of the criminal justice system have increased by more than 600 percent (while public education spending grew by only 25 percent in real dollars). More than half of inmates are functionally illiterate and 40 percent of adjudicated juveniles have learning disabilities that were not diagnosed or treated in school.[22] States end up paying $30,000 per inmate to keep young men behind bars when they are unwilling to provide even a quarter of this cost to give them good schools. Increasingly, this growing strain on the economy is deflecting resources away from the services that could make people pro-

23

ductive. California and Massachusetts had the dubious distinction this year of paying as much for prisons as for higher education.

Meanwhile, many are losing touch with the futures that would have enabled them to be contributing members of society. Take, for instance, the case of twenty-year-old Tracey Newhart of Falmouth, Massachusetts, who left school in 2003 without a diploma because she could not pass one part of the MCAS exam on repeated attempts. Although Newhart has Down's syndrome, a chromosome disorder that causes mental retardation, last year she won an award in a cooking competition, beating local caterers. Having worked hard to pass her classes throughout fifteen years of school, she had pinned her hopes on attending culinary school. Her dream dashed, Tracey joined 4,300 other Massachusetts seniors who failed the exam after multiple attempts, 40 percent of whom are special needs students, along with an estimated 11,000 students who had already dropped out of school since ninth grade, discouraged by their inability to pass the single high-stakes test that determines whether they can join the labor market and go on to become productive citizens in life.

Fixing NCLB

If we are to achieve the noble goals of NCLB, the law must be amended so that states have flexibility and encouragement to use thoughtful performance assessments and that tests are used diagnostically for informing curriculum improvements rather than for punishing students or schools. Progress should be evaluated on multiple measures—including such factors as attendance, school progress and continuation, course passage, and classroom performance on tasks beyond multiple choice tests. And gains should be evaluated with "value-added" measures showing how individual students improve over time, rather than school averages that are influenced by changes in who is assessed.

Targets should be based on sensible goals for student learning that also ensure appropriate assessment for special education students and English language learners and credit for the gains these students make over time. While progress for subgroups of students should be reported, these reports should include evidence about continuation and success in school, as well as academic achievement for members of each group. Determinations of school progress should be constructed to reflect a better grounded analysis of schools' actual performance and progress rather than a statistical gauntlet that penalizes schools serving the most diverse populations. These reporting changes should be designed to ensure that schools identified as failing are indeed those that are offering poor education, not those merely caught in a mathematical mousetrap. And progress should be gauged against sensible benchmarks for success. As policy analyst Bruce Fuller notes of the law's current 100 percent proficiency standard:

> Would government ever require automakers to produce emissions-free cars in the space of a decade, then shut down companies that failed to meet a pie-in-the-sky goal? Of course not! Better to set demanding yet pragmatic standards and require clear signs of progress. Schools should be rewarded for elevating achievement levels by some degree, rather than penalized for not meeting an absolute, unrealistic standard. The ideal level of proficiency for all—just like emissions-free cars—could then be approached gradually, over time.[23]

Most important, schools that are struggling should receive intensive help to strengthen their staffs and adopt successful programs. Full funding of NCLB should include support to hire well-qualified teachers and to provide intensive professional development: learning how to better teach those who struggle to learn. Full federal funding should also be used to leverage state investment, requiring the creation of Opportunity to Learn standards that can support annual reporting about the resources (teacher qualifications, curriculum opportunities, materials and equipment) available to children in all schools and annual progress on these indicators as well as indicators of student learning. Accountability must be two-way: state and federal support for ensuring qualified teachers and well-resourced schools must accompany expectations of students and schools.

Just offering high-stakes tests does not provide what parents and children would call genuine accountability. Obviously, students will not learn at higher levels unless they experience good teaching, a strong curriculum, and adequate resources. Most of the students who are struggling are students who have long experienced suboptimal schooling and students who have special learning needs that require higher levels of expertise from teachers. Because this nation has not yet invested heavily in teachers and their knowledge, the capacity to teach all students to high levels is not widespread. Only by investing in teaching can we improve the instruction of students who are currently struggling to learn; just adding tests and punishments will not do the trick.

Ensuring Qualified Teachers

One of the greatest shortcomings of schools serving our neediest students is that they typically have the least experienced and well-qualified teachers, even though such students need our most skilled teachers if they are to learn what they need to know. While recent studies have found that teacher quality is one of the most important school variables influencing stu-

dent achievement, teachers are the most inequitably distrib-
uted school resource. Although states do not allow the hiring of doctors, lawyers, or engineers who have not met licens-
ing standards, about thirty states still allow the hiring of
untrained teachers who do not meet their certification standards, most of them are assigned to teach the most disadvantaged students in low-income and high-minority schools, and
the most highly educated teachers are typically hired by
wealthier schools.[24]

One of the great ironies of the federal education programs
designed to support the education of low-income students
and those requiring special education, compensatory education, or bilingual education services is that poor schools have
often served these students with unqualified teachers and
untrained aides, rather than the highly skilled teachers envisioned by federal laws. The very purpose of the legislation—to
ensure greater opportunities for learning for these students—
has often been undermined by local inability to provide them
with teachers who have the skills to meet their needs.

In states that have lowered standards rather than increasing incentives to teaching, it is not hard to find urban and
poor rural schools where one-third or more of the teachers
are working without training, certification, or mentoring. In
schools with the highest minority enrollments, students have
less than a 50 percent chance of getting a mathematics or science teacher with a license and a degree in the field that they
teach. Thus, students who are the least likely to have learning
supports at home are also least likely to have teachers who
understand how children learn and develop, who know how
to teach them to read and problem solve, and who know what
to do if they are having difficulty.

Thus, one of the most important aspects of No Child Left
Behind is that it requires all schools to provide "highly qualified teachers" to all students by 2006. This requirement—that

all teachers be fully certified and show competence in the subject areas they teach—is intended to correct this long-standing problem. And it is a problem that can be solved. What often looks like a teacher shortage is actually mostly a problem of getting teachers from where they are trained to where they are needed and keeping teachers in the profession, especially in central cities and poor rural areas. More than 30 percent of beginners leave teaching within five years, and low-income schools suffering from even higher turnover rates, producing more teachers—especially through fast-track routes that tend to have high attrition—is like spending all our energy filling a leaky bucket rather than fixing it.

We need to understand this problem if we are to solve it. There are actually at least three or four times as many credentialed teachers in the United States as there are jobs, and many states and districts have surpluses. Not surprisingly, teachers are less likely to enter and stay in teaching where salaries are lower and working conditions are poorer. They are also more than twice as likely to leave if they have not had preparation for teaching and if they do not receive mentoring in their early years on the job. These are problems that can be solved. States and districts that have increased and equalized salaries to attract qualified teachers, have created strong preparation programs so that teachers are effective with the students they will teach, and have provided mentors show how we can fill classrooms with well-prepared teachers.

But solving this problem everywhere requires a national agenda. The distributional inequities that lead to the hiring of unqualified teachers are caused not only by disparities in pay and working conditions, but also by interstate barriers to teacher mobility, inadequate recruitment incentives to distribute teachers appropriately, and fiscal conditions that often produce incentives for hiring the least expensive rather than the most qualified teachers. And while the nation actually produces far more new teachers than it needs, some specific teaching fields experience real shortages. These include teachers for children with disabilities and those with limited English proficiency, as well as teachers of science and mathematics. Boosting supply in the fields where there are real shortfalls requires targeted recruitment and investment in the capacity of preparation institutions to expand their programs to meet national needs in key areas.

Although No Child Left Behind sets an expectation for hiring qualified teachers, it does not yet include the policy support to make this possible. The federal government should play a leadership role in providing an adequate supply of well-qualified teachers just as it has in providing an adequate supply of well-qualified physicians for the nation. When shortages of physicians were a major problem more than forty years ago, Congress passed the 1963 Health Professions Education Assistance Act to support and improve the caliber of medical training, create and strengthen teaching hospitals, provide scholarships and loans to medical students, and implement incentives for physicians to train in shortage specialties and locate in underserved areas. Similar federal initiatives in education were effective during the 1960s and 1970s but were eliminated in the 1980s. We need a federal teacher policy that will (1) *recruit new teachers* who prepare to teach in high-need fields and locations, through scholarships and forgivable loans that allow them to receive high-quality teacher education; (2) *strengthen teachers' preparation* through incentive grants to schools of education to create professional development schools, like teaching hospitals, to train prospective teachers in urban areas and to expand and improve programs to prepare special education teachers, teachers of English language learners, and other areas where our needs exceed our current capacity; and (3) *improve teacher retention and effectiveness* by ensuring they have mentoring

LINDA DARLING-HAMMOND

support during the beginning stage when 30 percent of them drop out of teaching.²⁵ For the cost of 1 percent of the Bush administration's 2003 tax cuts or the equivalent of one week's combat costs during the war in Iraq, we could provide top-quality preparation for more than 150,000 new teachers to teach in high-need schools and mentor all of the new teachers who are hired over the next five years. With just a bit of focus, we could ensure that all students in the United States are taught by highly qualified teachers within the next five years. Now that would be *real* accountability.

In addition to incentives for recruiting and retaining high-quality teachers in the places where they are most needed, fixing No Child Left Behind will require a new approach to measuring and supporting school success. This approach should, first, fix the accountability provisions of the law by:

- *Replacing the counterproductive federally mandated AYP formula with less rigid and more instructionally useful state accountability systems designed to 1) support and assess student progress on thoughtful assessments; 2) reduce achievement gaps among groups of students; and 3) increase graduation rates.*

- *Encouraging rather than discouraging the use of diagnostic assessments and high-quality state or local performance assessments as a key part of state accountability systems aimed at improving curriculum and teaching rather than punishing students or schools.*

- *Including multiple measures of learning and progress in assessing school progress and success, not just standardized tests—as well as results of performance assessments, attendance, and student continuation in and progress through school.*

- Evaluating gains using "value-added" approaches that assess the progress of individual students, not changes in average student scores that penalize schools which serve the neediest students or encourage schools to keep out or push out low-scoring students

- Assessing the progress of English language learners and students with disabilities based on professional testing standards and "counting" the gains of these students throughout their entire school careers, rather than counting only for the time they are "classified" in these categories.

Even more important, the law should improve the quality of education students actually receive by:

- Fully funding NCLB and developing a major federal initiative to underwrite strong preparation and recruitment incentives for well-qualified teachers who will teach in high-need schools.

- Ensuring that states focus attention and expertise on truly failing schools and that federal funding is organized to direct substantial resources toward the core building blocks of school success—the provision of well-qualified teachers, small classes, strong curriculum, and high-quality materials—rather than offering only supplemental services and an unusable transfer option.

- Leveraging more adequate and equitable state funding of public schools by requiring states to report and monitor school progress on Opportunity to Learn standards that reveal resources available to children (teacher qualifications, curriculum opportunities, materials and equipment) alongside their publication of achievement data.

At the heart of these reforms must be a recognition that public education is in many ways the very foundation of our democracy and *the* public institution that defines the people's concept of "public." It is the nation's most valuable public resource for creating common ground in what we as a collective know and believe, for developing a strong citizenry, and for ensuring a prepared workforce. It serves as the center of all types of communities and as the glue that holds us together as a people. Although there is a strong privatization instinct in Washington at the moment, the American people reiterate in poll after poll that they support public education, are willing to invest in it, and expect it to be leavening agent for society—in fact, some might argue, the only one left in America. While there are improvements to be made in schools, schools are a product of the society we have jointly created and will meet the aspirations Americans hold for them only if they are given intelligent guidance and the critical supports they need, while children are assured the health and family supports that allow them to be ready to learn.

Unfortunately, the NCLB law does not provide those supports and, poorly administered, has the potential to undermine successful schools while failing to fix or re-create those that are truly failing. Meanwhile, NCLB could damage the ability of public education to play its critical and vital role in our society. If we really care about Leave No Child Behind, our policies should invest in public schools in all communities; encourage teaching and assessment that supports higher-order thinking and performance; and create "two-way accountability"—accountability to parents and children for the quality of education they receive—as a means for greater learning for all.

2: A View from the Field: NCLB's Effects on Classrooms and Schools

GEORGE WOOD

I share the following story with no great sense of pride. This past January I met with our school's guidance counselor about Angelica. Angelica had come to us in an unusual way: her father, living at an address we could not verify but were pretty sure was not in our school district, had arranged for a friend who lived in our district to "take care" of her. Today we were meeting to deal with the continuing saga of Angelica's life. Not only was she failing all the classes she was taking, we could not get records from her former school because of school fees she owed. While nice enough in school, Angelica wasn't doing any work and we were uncertain if, at age sixteen, she had ever passed a high school class. Along with Angelica, her advisor, her father, and Children's Protective Services, we arrived at a plan to keep her in school.

But not before one unvoiced thought occurred to me as principal...if we just sent her back to her home school she wouldn't count on our records. Angelica was likely not to graduate on time, hadn't passed the state-mandated graduation tests, and had spotty attendance. Every one of those indicators would count against our school on our state report card, even though Angelica had only attended our school for less than a year. And our report card, based primarily on test scores, would determine whether or not we continued to operate without state intervention. In a real sense I was being asked to choose between the school and the child.

While we did not send Angelica away, that the thought of such an action would occur to me in my role as principal is a logical, though unfortunate, consequence of the standards and testing movement in this country and of the No Child Left Behind Act in particular. For nearly twenty years we have ventured down this radical path of school reform that has led to more students being pushed out of school, more retentions of students, more dropouts, a narrowing of the curricula, and dissatisfaction on the part of teachers, students, and parents. NCLB, which institutionalizes these narrow and inaccurate measures of school performance in unprecedented ways, only makes it worse.

Throughout this book many of the failings of NCLB are laid out, from the movement of resources away from needy schools and children to the control over schools given over to federal bureaucrats to the lack of appropriate funding—to name but a few. But for me the most devastating effects of the bill are seen in our classrooms. As a high school principal who also works with schools nationwide, married to a kindergarten teacher, I have experienced firsthand what NCLB leaves behind—and it is the notion that schools have any role aside from preparing our children to take tests.

The reliance on standardized test data in appraising the quality or worth of our schools and children is nothing new. Even without the new testing requirements found in NCLB, nineteen states (with over half of our public school students) had in place graduation tests by 2003 with five more states slated to have them by 2008. Additionally, dozens of states were regularly testing elementary school children for promotion and ranked the quality of their schools by test scores. The advent of NCLB accelerated this trend, with every state that accepts federal dollars being required to test students annually in grades three through eight and once in high school in reading and mathematics, with science tests phased in by 2008. Scores on these tests must improve yearly (making what is called Adequate Yearly Progress, AYP) to all students reaching proficiency by 2014; if they do not, the school faces sanctions, ranging from having to pay for students to go to other schools to the dismissal of the school faculty and administration. Tests designed merely to provide diagnostic information might in theory be harmless, even useful. But I want to show that high-stakes tests that serve as the principal or only measure of school performance and have sever sanctions attached are actively harmful to the project of teaching and learning in schools.

Given that the pressure to raise test scores has been on our schools for a while, we can see the damage these tests have already wrought on our children and their classrooms. I have searched in vain to find any study that says our children graduate as better employees, college students, or citizens as a result of taking more tests. In fact, the only evidence that things are improving as a result of testing is that test scores are gradually going up. This is no surprise and only points out the fallacy of confusing measuring our schools with improving them—the goal has become simply higher test scores, with no evidence that these scores translate into post-school success. Indeed, there is abundant reason to believe that the skills needed to do well on these tests at best reflect a shallow kind of learning and at worst indicate only a better ability to take tests.[1]

However, there is growing evidence that virtually all the effects of the tactics used to raise test scores have been negative. This includes the pushing out, retention, and dropping out of students who do not test well; the narrowing of the curriculum and classroom practices; and the limiting of the school experience. These have been the costs of our growing reliance on standardized tests as measures of our schools, and, with the NCLB upping the ante for schools when it comes to these scores, we should expect to see even harsher consequences for our schools, kids, and communities. From research and news reports, field observations, and my own work as a principal, here is a limited accounting of these trends—watch for them in a school near you.

School Pushouts, Dropouts, and Retentions

Let's start with the most obvious case: Houston, Texas. As noted in the introduction to this book, Houston is the home of the oft-cited "Texas miracle" upon which much of the NCLB legislation is based. Houston has won numerous awards for meeting the strict Texas testing standards; in particular, the district claimed a dropout rate of 1.5 percent and won acclaim for dramatically improving tenth-grade test scores. Administrators received bonuses, citations and plaques were handed out, and civil leaders patted themselves on the back. Not only had schools improved, they had done so with very little additional money. It was, as exposed by reports in the *New York Times* and on CBS News, simply too good to be true.

In fact, at Houston's Sharpston High School, 463 of its 1,700 students left during the 2001–2002 school year but not one was reported as a dropout. Rather, when they left they were assigned numerical codes that claimed they had changed schools, gone for a G.E.D., or returned to their native country—when many of them never told the school authorities any such thing. In reality the dropout rate in Houston is thought to be somewhere between 33 and 50 percent.

Houston is not an isolated phenomenon. In cities across

the country similar reports pop up almost daily in the press and we are seeing more of them as NCLB standards begin to be implemented. New York papers have accused that city of using "Enron accounting" when it comes to reporting test scores and dropouts. In Massachusetts, claims of a 93 percent statewide graduation rate have been challenged by data that demonstrates that only 71 percent of the kids that started ninth grade actually cross the stage at graduation. Reports such as these illustrate the fact that there has been a falling graduation rate nationwide, correlated to the increasing number of standardized tests students must take.[2]

Much of this fall in real graduation numbers can be correlated with a similar rise in the number of students being retained in grade level for more than one year. There is little educational research as conclusive as that on school retention. The evidence is clear—when students are retained in the same grade for more than one year the likelihood that they will drop out rises dramatically. While students have always been retained, retention seems to be reaching epidemic proportions. Nationwide there is a growing bulge of students in the ninth grade, leading, not surprisingly, to a growing rate of student attrition between ninth and tenth grades.[3]

What does testing have to do with this? First, states are now retaining, by law, elementary students if they do not pass a standardized test, usually one in reading. Flying in the face of all the clear evidence on how children learn to read at different ages, the test and measure pattern of one-size-test-fits-all puts children who come to reading later in peril of being retained. With older students, schools are actually holding students back in grade so that they *avoid* taking the mandated tests and the school's overall passing rate looks better. Stories such as that of Perla A., one of what is thought to be as many as 60 percent of Houston ninth graders retained to avoid a tenth grade test, is not unusual:

> Perla passed all her courses save one, Algebra, in ninth grade.
> But when she returned the following year she was told she would
> repeat the same grade and courses. Protesting, she was told by
> her counselor, "Don't worry about it . . . I'm just doing my job."
> She spent three years in ninth grade, finally passing Algebra in
> summer school and being promoted right to eleventh grade—
> past the tenth grade and the all-important test. Lacking the cred-
> its to graduate, she dropped out.[4]

When schools are judged on how well students test, students not likely to succeed are encouraged not to test or are
simply asked to leave school. Schools, according to Illinois education superintendent Robert Schiller, are pressured to push
out truant or low-performing students in order to meet demands to improve test scores. (Witness the growing number
of dropouts in Chicago, up to 17,400 in the 2001–2002 school
year.)[5] And, according to Schiller, the increasing pressure to
move students out of school is being increased by the provisions of NCLB.

This pressure on students comes in the form of encouraging their absence, moving them to another school, or just
pushing them out of school altogether. Usually this happens
to students least able to defend themselves from this pressure, students like Angelica at my school and Perla in Houston. Children who lack the family support necessary to fight
back, children who are often poor, handicapped, or of color—
precisely those children NCLB was created to protect.

Classroom Practices

It should not be news to anyone that teachers across the country, either by choice or in response to administrative pressures, are teaching to the tests. Why shouldn't they? When

test scores are all that matter, when they determine if children advance from grade to grade or even graduate, test preparation is the order of the day. And it works, as demonstrated by research studies on college admissions test preparation programs (or simply attested to by the millions of dollars spent on that industry). But at what cost?

Teachers across the map complain that the joy is being drained from teaching as their work is reduced to passing out worksheets and drilling children as if they were in dog obedience school. Elementary "test prep" classroom methods involve teachers snapping their fingers at children to get responses, following scripted lessons where they simply recite prompts for students or have children read nonsense books, devoid of plot or meaning. One Ohio teacher in a school that uses SRA's "Direct Instruction" model (perhaps better called instructional destruction) describes how she is now expected to teach reading through following a set "script":

> I am to point to a letter in a word, say, for example, "not." The script tells me to point to the first letter and sing out "Ready, what sound?" Then I point to one of the children who is to give me the "n" sound. I am to repeat this with each letter, then say "Ready, what word?" and as I glide my finger under the entire word the children are to miraculously put the sounds together and read. She demonstrates this from a 200-page book where each lesson she is to teach is completely scripted out—the teachers also had to attend several days of training, apparently to learn how to read the instructions and to be prevented from changing any of them.

After enough words can be successfully decoded by the children, a "story book" is presented. Here, in its entirety, is a story that children might get to read from the kindergarten "story book." (Lack of capitalization in the original.)

> *a girl in a cave*
>
> *a girl was in a cave. a wave came in the cave. the girl said, "save me, save me."*
>
> *a fish came in the cave. she said, "I will save that girl." and she did.*
>
> *the fish said, "now I will give that girl a seed and a ham to eat." so she gave the girl a seed and a ham.*[6]

And, by the way, the children are taught only the letter sounds at this level, not the names of the letters, because it might confuse them—even though the names of letters are on the standardized tests. In order to boost the skills found on standardized tests—those being the lowest-level reading skills—good literature and meaningful stories are being banished from classrooms around the country. Who would have thought we would long for the days of Dick and Jane?

At the high school level teachers race to cover mountains of content, hoping their charges will memorize the right terms for true/false or multiple choice exams. There can be no time for exploring the roots of the war in Iraq when students will face tests asking them to choose between the definitions of "despotism" and "absolute dictatorship." While it might be possible to teach some of these terms and other items in the context of world issues the sheer number required by testing standards prohibits taking the time to do so.

For example, in New York City, history teacher Dalia Hochman points out that teaching history has become a race to cover everything that might be on the test. "In one stretch we do the scientific revolution, French revolution, revolution in Haiti, Simon Bolivar and Latin American independence movements, the Napoleonic period, ninteenth-century nationalism in Italy and Germany, Zionism, and back to the Industrial Revolution—it's a race to the finish."

Not confined to dumbing down humanities teaching, National Academy of Sciences President Bruce Alberts has said that science education in America is in decline—the culprit, standardized testing. "Everyone wants accountability but it's easier to test for facts than understanding." Alberts goes on to note that as children progress through elementary school science classes are reduced to "memorizing thirty different kinds of whales and then spitting out that information." This, he contends, will only get worse when NCLB requires nationwide science testing in 2008.[7]

From Dalia Hochman's classroom, here is how this press to test effects teachers:

> Hochman of La Guardia High, a 2000 Yale graduate in history, spent a recent weekend writing comments on 170 term papers that examined an international response to a world problem—like AIDS in Uganda. The papers were brilliant and deep, she says, but it bothers her that they are not part of the state evaluation of her students or her school. Though she loves their lively classroom discussions, she feels constant pressure to cut it off, to keep up with a test-driven curriculum that, she believes, goes a mile wide and an inch deep. After Sept. 11, 2001, her students begged for special lessons on Islam . . . (but) she said, a veteran mentor teacher warned her, "Honey, spend two days on the Byzantine Empire and three days on Islam, and then you've go to move on."
>
> And though she has bright students (virtually all pass the state test) so much is crammed in . . . "it's unbelievable how little they remember a year later." Several sophomores she had for global history are now juniors in her American history class. "When we got to World War I, they said, 'Is that the one with Mussolini?'"[8]

As the pressure to raise test scores increases under NCLB stories like these will only multiply.

Narrowing the School Experience

School people are no fools. Tell them what they will be measured on and they will try to measure up. What this has meant for the curriculum and the school day is that test preparation crowds out much else that parents have taken for granted in their schools.

Horror stories abound beginning with our youngest of students. On September 19, 2003, five-year-old kindergartners took their last schooltime nap in Gadsden, Alabama. Nap time, the district's administrators had decided, would be eliminated to make more time for test preparation. "If the state is holding us accountable, this is the way we have to do it," said Wynell Williams, elementary education director for the Gadsden School System. "Kindergarten is not like it used to be."[9] No kidding.

Not to be outdone, the Galveston, Texas, schools took away recess time to make more room for instruction. According to published reports, parents claim their children "get less personal break time each week than office workers get on coffee breaks." Responding to these claims, one principal pointed out that students and teachers are under pressure to pass Texas state-mandated tests. "I guess it would be easy for me to say we should have more recess, but unless we add time to each day to do it, we have to make use of our instructional time to make sure our kids are prepared." If this was limited to one city we could blame it on overzealous administrators. But in fact more and more schools are cutting back on unstructured playtime for children and schools are now being built without playgrounds.[10]

Remember field trips? Sure, some were a waste of time, but when done well they made real-world connections with what was learned in school. Not anymore, according to Kristan Von Wald, head of the Association for Experiential Education. Commenting on the declining number of such experiences she notes that "anything that doesn't directly contribute to higher test scores will be scrutinized very carefully."[11] That includes not just field trips, but sometimes entire programs. In one Florida community the entire agriculture program was threatened with closure due to pressure to provide more academic time to help students pass the FCAT, the Florida Comprehensive Assessment Test, a test that determines Florida's compliance with NCLB.[12] This scenario is repeated in district after district with art, music, shop, and other "elective" programs—often the very programs that keep kids connected with and in school.

All of this is summed up in the experience of one Iowa school. When threatened with NCLB sanctions they responded:

> Here are some of the things kids at Garfield/Franklin elementary in Muscatine, Iowa, no longer do: eagle watch on the Mississippi River, go on field trips to the University of Iowa's Museum of Natural History, and have two daily recesses. . . . Creative writing, social studies and computer work have all become occasional indulgences. Now that the standardized fill-in-the-bubble test is the foundation upon which the public schools rest—now that a federal law called No Child Left Behind mandates that kids as young as nine meet benchmarks in reading and math or jeopardize their school's reputation—there is little time for anything else.
>
> Franklin is one of the new law's success stories. After landing on the dreaded Schools in Need of Improvement list two years ago, the students and staff clawed their way off of it. . . . Last year Franklin was removed from "the bad list," as one child calls it. Through rote drills, one-on-one test talks and rigorous analysis of students' weaknesses, Franklin has become a reluctant model for the rest of the nation.[13]

Was this really the model of education we hoped for from NCLB?

If it wasn't bad enough that testing is shoving so much out the school door, think what it also lets in. When the only measure of a student or a school's success that matters is a test score, it is amazing what lengths schools will go to raise it. Take the case of the Racine, Wisconsin, schools. At Case High, to encourage kids to show up for the Wisconsin Knowledge and Concepts Examinations (WKCEs), the school gives out movie passes and enters students in drawings for shirts, etc. Other high schools up the ante, offering televisions and DVD players in their drawings. Gifford Elementary fourth graders are enticed to attend during test week with offers of more recess, movie privileges, and treats when a class has perfect attendance during test week. And across the state students were offered exemption from final exams if they do well enough on the WKCEs to earn the school a good NCLB rating.[14]

Is all this—kids pushed out of school, teaching and curriculum narrowed to "drill and kill" practices, school days without naps, recess or field trips, and testing days turned into *Let's Make A Deal*—what we want for our children? But who can blame the schools for making such deals with the devil when their ability to even be a school hangs on small percentage point shifts in test scores? What have we done to the experience of school in America? We have embarked on one of the greatest social engineering experiments ever to be conducted on our children. With no evidence of producing better citizens, neighbors, employees, or college students, we are testing our children at a rate never before known in our society. And we are using these tests to sort and label our kids and our schools. It has been a multibillion-dollar gamble with nothing at all to show for it to date.

*   *   *

If these have been the outcomes to date from the movement to hold our schools accountable primarily for higher standardized test score gains, should we expect anything different as NCLB continues to be phased in? Not only do these experiences illustrate precisely what will happen in schools that face this testing pressure for the first time under NCLB, specific additional features of NCLB will make the effects of testing even more counterproductive. In particular, the threats to schools requiring that they transfer students, fund after school programs (sometimes provided by private outside agencies) from already limited dollars, remove existing teachers and administrators, and potentially come under state control will focus even more attention on the tests. Sadly, it is upon the children in the very schools NCLB was designed to help that the greatest blows will fall.

Passed with great fanfare as a "civil rights" agenda—attempting to focus on the achievement gap, the gap between the rich and poor, minority and majority children when it comes to test scores—many hoped that schools for our most needy children would improve. And yet it is these same schools, which attempt to serve these children, that will be the most vulnerable to NCLB sanctions. Since NCLB is unaccompanied by any attempt to close any other "gaps" our children face, which is pointed out by Stan Karp in chapter 3 of this book, schools that serve the poor will face a greater burden in meeting NCLB goals. Additionally, in a country where some schools that serve well-to-do children in prosperous neighborhoods spend as much as three times more per child as schools in urban or rural settings, we should simply expect that schools serving the neediest students will do the poorest under NCLB standards. NCLB as well as the policies of our federal and state governments are silent on these gaps, but these same policies will punish severely those who attempt to close them.

NCLB is set up to penalize schools that actually do attempt to make a difference for our poor and minority students. In this, the second year of NCLB, schools with more diverse populations are being punished by NCLB. Called the "diversity penalty," this phenomenon occurs because the greater the diversity in a school the more likely the school will fail to meet AYP. (Remember that failing to meet AYP means that schools will be punished.) This is because of a specific feature of the legislation which says that if just one so-called subgroup fails to meet the standard, the entire school fails. For example, in one Florida school district a school previously judged to be outstanding suddenly found itself rated as failing even though 80 percent of its students were judged to be proficient in math and 88 percent in reading. The reason for the failing score was that a group of 45 special education students, out of a population of 1,150 students, failed to improve their test scores. But a neighboring school, with 39 special education students, did not have the scores of these students counted—because there have to be 40 students in any subgroup to be measured.[15] Clearly the more subgroups a school tries to serve, groups that are defined by racial or income status, the greater the likelihood that the school will not make AYP.

It is not only schools with multiple subgroups that suffer under NCLB. Looking at schools in Ohio that have been named as the 2003–2004 "Blue Ribbon" high schools under the NCLB standards, we find that when compared to the average high school in Ohio, the State NCLB Blue Ribbon Schools:

- *Spend 17 percent more per student than state average per-pupil spending*

- *Have a low teacher-student ratio (1:15)*

- Are not diverse (with fewer than 2 percent minority students compared to a state average of 21.3 percent)

- Have virtually no poor students (2 percent compared to the state's 29 percent)

- Have few special education students (7.7 percent compared to 13.3 percent)

- Pay teachers in excess of $10,000 more than state average

- Have a low student mobility rate (2.4 percent)

What could be clearer than that NCLB standards will most likely be met by well-funded districts with few children of color or special needs? Was this the intent of the law?

Since NCLB judges schools solely on test scores, schools that have students who do poorly on these tests will face the greatest pressure to focus on the tests. This means that schools who serve children who are poor, have limited English skills, require special education services, or are recent immigrants to this country, for example, have the most incentive to carry out the practices identified earlier—pushing out students, narrowing teaching and the curriculum, limiting the school experience. Perhaps the most detailed study to date of how such a reliance on test scores has affected schools serving our neediest children comes from the "birthplace" of NCLB, the state of Texas. Authored by Linda McNeil and Angela Valenzula, the study points out how the rush to test and measure has, in the case of Texas schools that serve disadvantaged Latino and African-American children, led to the following:

Reducing the quality and quantity of curriculum.

Distorting educational expenditures, diverting scarce instructional dollars away from such high-quality curricular resources as laboratory supplies and books to test-prep materials and activities of limited instructional value.

Provoking instruction aimed at the lowest level of skills and information, which crowds out other forms of learning, particularly for poor and minority students.

Teaching and test-prep practices that violate what is known about how children learn.

Widening the gap between the education of children in Texas's poorest (historically low-performing) schools and schools available to more privileged children.[16]

Experience tells us that in the name of raising test scores, the very things that children of limited means require for a full and rich school experience will be taken away from them. And all in the name of a law that claims to help these children.

What is to be done? Educators, parents, and students need to come together to challenge what is happening to the daily quality of school life for our children as a result of the pressure on testing. We seem to have accepted these tests as a fact of life when in fact they are only a recent development with no proven history. And now we have for the first time a federal law that mandates this unproven measure of our schools as the arbiter of what counts as a quality education.

To change this law will require a strategy that slows the progress of the standards and testing agenda and at the same time offers ways to focus on helping schools, especially those that serve our most vulnerable children. Strategies for such a national campaign could include the following:

Testing Moratorium. Call for a national or state-by-state moratorium on high-stakes testing until such tests can be established as having predictive value. That is, unless we can link test scores to some measure of success after leaving school they should not be given. Why deny a child a diploma or grade promotion, or teachers their jobs, if the tests used for these decisions cannot predict future success or measure the effectiveness of the schools? So far, no such evidence has been forthcoming, even as we pour billions of dollars into testing and threaten students, their families, and teachers with dire consequences based on these scores.

Assessments of School Health. A one time test does not really tell us what we want to know about our children or our schools. Parents and communities want schools where children are engaged, use their minds well, and yes, are even happy. Surveys of parents are clear; they want their children to be safe, to develop positive attitudes, to learn to be responsible citizens. A measure of school health would take into account all of this, and a richer sense of academic achievement (including samples of student work and demonstrations of competency). The federal government should launch, in concert with states that were already started down this path, a major research and design campaign to develop just such an assessment, as outlined by Monty Neill in chapter 6 of this book.

Targeted Intervention. Clearly many public schools are failing; and many communities and states are failing their schools. We don't need another set of tests to show us that. What we do need is to target intervention funds and support to schools that serve large numbers of our poor or disadvantaged students. We should begin by demanding that funding for our schools be not only equalized but that additional funds should flow to schools that serve our most needy students. To hold schools accountable without appropriate support is worse than farce, it is a tragedy. Additionally, this targeted support should promote and enable proven strategies for improving student attendance, engagement, and the expansion of academic success. For example, the work going on in our major cities today to break up larger schools is based on years of experience with urban school success, as are the teaching assessment practices that are carried out in these schools. Ironically, while millions are poured into testing, the most recent federal budget proposals have eliminated all funding to the Small Learning Communities initiative that has supported this work.

Many of the supporters of the NCLB have good intentions, hoping for schools to work even harder to meet the needs of our children. Unfortunately their intentions have been hijacked by a one-size-fits-all, blame-and-shame agenda that will do nothing to help our schools and will only exacerbate an already unfortunate trend. By offering alternatives that build on those intentions and celebrate rather than castigate our system of public education we may find ourselves on the road to leaving no child, school, family, or community behind.

PART TWO

NCLB in a Larger Context

3: NCLB's Selective Vision of Equality: Some Gaps Count More than Others

STAN KARP

Thanks to No Child Left Behind, AYP's have been replacing the ABC's as the most important letters in many schools.

AYP, or "adequate yearly progress," refers to the formulas that the No Child Left Behind Act (NCLB) uses to evaluate schools on the basis of standardized test scores. Under NCLB, all schools receiving federal funds are required to reach 100 percent passing rates for all student groups on state tests by the 2013–2014 school year. The declared goal is to have all students meet state standards and to eliminate academic achievement gaps.

This new mandate—which as shown below is both restrictive and seriously underfunded—is now the main preoccupation of districts and schools across the country. NCLB sets up an elaborate system of federally mandated testing with as many as forty different test score targets for each school. Any school that misses even one of these targets for two consecutive years faces an escalating series of sanctions, from the loss of federal funds to the imposition of private management on public schools or even possible closure.

Yet the goal of equality in test scores for all student groups, including special education and bilingual students, contrasts sharply with the widespread inequality that is tolerated, or even promoted, by federal policy in many other areas. NCLB imposes a mandate on schools that is put on no other institution in society: wipe out inequalities while the factors that help produce them remain in place. A closer look at this contradiction sheds light on why critics see NCLB as part of a calculated political campaign to use achievement gaps to label schools as failures, without providing the resources and strategies needed to overcome them.

But, first, let's take a closer look at how AYP works. AYP is the rate of improvement schools must make on their state test scores to reach 100 percent within the allowed time frame. Schools must meet separate AYP targets for up to ten different student categories (total school population, special education students, Limited English Proficiency students, whites, African Americans, Asian/Pacific Islanders, Native Americans, Hispanics, other ethnicities, and economically disadvantaged students).

In each category there are two mandates: 95 percent of the students in each group must take the test, and each group must make its annual AYP target, which is the steadily rising percentage of passing students needed to stay on pace to reach 100 percent by 2014. Multiply this by the number of federally mandated tests, currently math and language arts, with science coming soon, and you have a dizzying obstacle course of hoops that schools must jump through.

Schools that miss any single target for two consecutive years get put on the "needs improvement" list and face sanctions. After two years, they must use federal funds to support student transfers. Three years brings "corrective action" and vouchers for supplemental tutorial services; four years brings "reconstitution," including replacement of school staff; five years brings "restructuring," which can mean anything from state takeover to imposing private management on public schools.

Supporters of NCLB claim that the tests and sanctions are the keys to bringing improvement and accountability to all schools. But the AYP system is an arbitrary and inappropriate assessment scheme that does not provide an accurate picture of how schools are serving their students, and the sanctions it imposes for low test scores have no record of success as school improvement strategies. These are not educational strategies at all, but political strategies designed to bring a kind of "market reform" to public education.

Under AYP, the only thing that counts is the number of students who score above the passing level on the state test. So on a test like New Jersey's High School Proficiency Assessment, where a passing score is 200, helping a bilingual special education student from a low-income household raise his/her test score from, say, 50 to 199 counts for nothing. In fact, such a score counts as a failure in four different subgroups. Moving a student from 199 to 200 is success.

This is just one example of the ridiculous ways NCLB uses state test scores as the sole measure of school and student progress. There are many others.

The larger and more culturally diverse a school is, the more likely it is to be labeled as inadequate by NCLB.[1] A racially and economically homogeneous school in the suburbs has many fewer hurdles to overcome than an urban school with large populations of special education, immigrant, or low-income students.

Another arbitrary variable is the size of subgroups a school must have before their scores count for AYP purposes. For example, Minnesota substantially reduced the number of schools on its "needs improvement" list when it changed the threshold for the number of special education students from

20 to 40.[2] Some research, however, suggests that any subgroup sample less than 70 is inherently unreliable.[3]

Moreover, all the sanctions in NCLB are triggered by year-to-year changes in standardized test scores. But researchers Thomas Kane and Douglas Staiger have shown that up to 70 percent of these changes can be caused by random fluctuation—things like variations in transient student population or statistical error in the tests themselves. "The AYP system cannot tell the difference between a learning gain and random noise," they concluded.[4]

The testing mandates for special education and Limited English Proficiency (LEP) students, in particular, are striking examples of AYP's counterproductive impact. While there is a legitimate argument to be made that leaving students out of high-stakes assessments encourages schools to overlook their needs, including them in a bad system like AYP pressures schools to modify special programs for these students in harmful ways.

For example, students are put into the LEP category precisely because they have not yet mastered the English skills required for grade-level academic work. Yet NCLB is forcing large numbers of LEP students to take content area tests in a language they don't understand and schools face penalties when the scores come up short.

In special education classes across the nation, NCLB is pressuring teachers to substitute an inappropriate focus on test-taking skills instead of serving the individual needs of the students in front of them. Some states, like Oregon, have given special education parents the right to determine when their children are ready to take state assessments, but under NCLB the federal government makes the choice for them. As a result, special ed students in some schools find themselves being blamed for the school's poor AYP results and for putting "good schools" on "the list."

If the federal government wanted to help special needs students it would fully fund the Individuals with Disabilities Education Act (IDEA), as called for repeatedly by education advocates. (The government currently provides less than half the federal funding authorized by the IDEA.)[5] It would also support effective bilingual education programs for English language learners and encourage assessment practices that promote content learning and language acquisition simultaneously. Instead, the new regulations will greatly restrict the use of effective bilingual education programs and promote a kind of "English only" intolerance.

Outcries over the testing mandates for special education and LEP students led the Department of Education to belatedly modify NLCB implementation regulations. But the revised regulations only marginally altered the AYP formulas for these students and did not fundamentally change their harmful impact.[6] In fact, the Department's lame response to such glaring flaws in NCLB underscores the difficulties involved in trying to transform NCLB from a "test and punish" law into a school improvement law.

In general, the massive increase in testing that NCLB will impose on schools will hurt their educational performances, not improve them. When schools become obsessed with test scores, they narrow the focus of what teachers do in classrooms and limit their ability to serve the broader needs of children and their communities. In many Philadelphia schools, students are reading fewer books to make more room for test prep. Baltimore schools are spending 20 percent less time on social studies, one of many subjects not on the mandated tests and therefore receiving less attention and fewer resources. Oregon is cutting foreign language and music classes and spending more on data collection and testing programs.[7]

Overreliance on testing diverts attention and resources from more promising school improvement strategies like smaller class size, creative curriculum reform, and collaborative professional development. High-stakes tests push struggling students out of school, and encourage schools to adopt developmentally inappropriate practices for younger children in an effort to "get them ready for the tests." Overuse of testing can also encourage cheating scandals and makes schools and students vulnerable to inaccurate and, at times, corrupt practices by commercial testing firms.

Tests alone do very little to increase the capacity of schools to deliver better educational services. They can also provide a kind of counterfeit accountability that sorts and labels kids on the basis of multiple-choice questions as a substitute for the much more difficult and more costly process of real school improvement. The keys to school improvement are not standards and tests, but teachers and students. And while teachers and students need a complicated mix of support, resources, motivation, pressure, leadership, and professional skills to succeed, the idea that this mixture can be provided by test-driven sanctions is simply wrong and is not supported by any educational research or real world experience.

Already 28,000 of the nation's 90,000 schools have been warned they are candidates for "the list," and estimates indicate that ultimately over 75 percent of all public schools will be labeled "in need of improvement."[8] The main effect will not be to promote school improvement or accountability, but to create a widespread public perception of systemic failure that will erode the common ground a universal system of public education needs to survive.

As this new federal testing scheme begins to document an inability to reach its unrealistic and underfunded goals, it will provide new ammunition for a push to fundamentally "overhaul" and reshape public schooling. Conservative pundits will press their critique of public education as a "failed monopoly" that must be "re-formed" through market measures, vouchers, and other steps toward privatization.

Many educators are understandably reluctant to oppose NCLB's noble-sounding goals and share concerns about persistent disparities in student achievement. But the AYP formulas and the "Leave No Child Behind" rhetoric of the new federal law are transparent attempts to set up schools to fail. By shining the spotlight on test score gaps, NCLB effectively invokes concerns about historic inequities and provides a platform for President Bush's posturing about the "soft bigotry of low expectations." But the real measure of such concern is what supporters of NCLB propose to do about this inequality, not only in schools, but in society as a whole. Here the record leaves little room for doubt: Inequality is as American as processed apple pie.

Take, for example, income inequality among some of the same groups NCLB says must reach 100 percent test score equality within twelve years. Education research has established a strong link between student performance on standardized tests and family income. While income inequality in a community is no excuse for school failure, certainly any serious federal plan to close academic achievement gaps needs to concern itself with trends in closely related areas, like the resources that families and schools have to work with.

But a look at the data on income inequality—especially through the prism of AYP—reveals the hypocrisy at the heart of the NCLB legislation. In 1991, the median household income for black families was about 58 percent of white income. Hispanic income was about 70 percent. If we applied the AYP system to this key measure of how our economy works, income gaps for blacks would have had to narrow by 3.5 percent each year to pull even within twelve years—the same time frame schools have been given to equalize test scores. Hispanics, starting with a smaller gap, would have had to close the gap by 2.5 percent a year.

But if you compare this to how the economy actually performed between 1991 and 2002, a period of supposedly unprecedented economic growth, you'll find the U.S. economy did not come anywhere near to making "adequate yearly progress" towards the goal of income equality. At the end of twelve years, the gap between black and white income had narrowed only a pitiful 3.7 percent; for Hispanics the gap was just .4 percent less than it was in 1991.[9]

If we lived in an alternate universe where income equality really was a goal of federal economic policy and an NCLB-like system of sanctions put pressure on the titans of industry and commerce to attain such a lofty goal, what might be appropriate remedies for such a dismal performance: "corrective action?" to borrow the language of NCLB sanctions; economic restructuring? reconstitution of our major corporations? How about "state takeover"?

The point, of course, is that there is no indicator of equality— including household income, child poverty rates, health care coverage, home ownership, or school spending—where federal policy currently mandates equality among all population groups within twelve years under threat of sanctions— except standardized test scores in public schools.

If this sounds unfair and absurd, that's because it is. Imagine a federal law that declared that 100 percent of all citizens must have adequate health care in twelve years or sanctions will be imposed on doctors and hospitals. Or all crime must be eliminated in twelve years or the local police department will face privatization.

Inequality in test scores is one indicator of school performance. But test scores also reflect other inequalities in resources and opportunities that exist in the larger society and in schools themselves. Ten percent of white children live in poverty, while about 30 percent of black and Latino children live in poverty. Students in poor schools, on average, have thousands of dollars less spent on their education than those in wealthier schools. About 10 percent of whites don't have health insurance, but 20 percent of blacks and over 30 percent of Latinos have no health insurance. Unemployment rates for blacks and Latinos are nearly double what they are for whites. [10]

Why are there no federal mandates demanding the elimination of these gaps? Don't these inequalities leave children behind?

In October 2003, the Educational Testing Service, the largest producer of standardized tests in the world and no hotbed of educational radicalism, issued a report on the achievement gap that tracked fourteen contributing factors, from birth weight and child nutrition to class size and teacher qualifications. The results were "unambiguous." The study found that, "In all 14 factors, the gaps in student achievement mirror inequalities in those aspects of school, early life, and home circumstances that research has linked to achievement."[11]

Yet, except for standardized test scores, none of these measures of inequality appear in the AYP charts used to label schools and impose penalties. Narrowly focusing in on test score gaps as the sole indicator of educational inequality is just one more way that standardized tests impose high-stakes consequences on the victims of educational failure rather than on those responsible for it.

Another study by the Economic Policy Institute (EPI) found that, "Before even entering kindergarten, the average cognitive scores of children in the highest SES [socioeconomic status] group are 60 percent above the scores of the lowest SES group."[12] Some of these differences are the direct result of highly preventable, but still pervasive, social and economic gaps. For example, in Detroit, African-American children under five have sixteen times the chance of being overexposed to lead than whites. Lead poisoning has dramatic and devastating effects on the academic potential of young children and has been effectively reduced in many areas. But in Detroit the black/white gap in the risk of lead exposure is twice the level that existed in the 1980s.[13] To allow this kind of inequality to grow, while mandating 100 percent equality in standardized test scores in Detroit public schools not only makes no sense educationally, is morally inexcusable.

As the EPI study put it, "As a nation, we continue to support the role—even the obligation—of schooling to close these gaps, but at the same we create or magnify the same gaps with other social policies. Except for continuing support for Head Start (actually a relatively inexpensive program), our public policies do little to address the negative educational effects that income disparities have on young children. The U.S. should not use one hand to blame the schools for inadequately serving disadvantaged children when its social policies have helped create these disadvantages—especially income disadvantages—with the other hand"[14]

NCLB does not even effectively promote equality in the area of school funding. The law does include some increases in federal funding for Title I schools and some modest efforts to redirect Title I funds to schools in the poorest communities. But these overdue, if inadequate, measures will be dwarfed by the impact of sanctions that require schools and districts to use up to 20 percent of their federal funds to support student transfers to other schools and provide vouchers for supplemental tutorial services. These sanctions, which again have no record of success as school improvement strategies, will actually reduce the funds available for school-wide reform in the affected schools.

The funding disparities built into the school finance system are an integral part of the race and class inequalities reflected in achievement gaps but overlooked by NCLB. A study by the Education Trust (a strong supporter of NCLB) has shown that "these gaps have real consequences for the quality of education low-income children receive. In North Dakota, which has the smallest gap, the $32-per-student difference between districts serving the most poor students and those serving the fewest translates into $12,800 for an elementary school of 400 students, enough to pay for a part-time reading specialist or buy 1,000 new books for the school library. At the other extreme, the equivalent $2,794-per-student gap in New York state translates into a whopping $1,117,600 for a 400-student elementary school, enough to compete with elite suburban schools for the most qualified teachers on the labor market and also provide extra instructional time for students who are behind."[15]

The gap between the promises NCLB makes and the funding it provides is even larger. Ever since the law passed in 2001, with overwhelming bipartisan support in both Houses of Congress, the media has been filled with complaints by Democrats who voted for NCLB that the Bush administration has not provided full funding for the law. And it's true that the administration's 2004 budget called for about $12 billion in funding instead of the $18 billion that Congress originally authorized. Much of the mainstream debate over NCLB has involved calls for "fully funding" the law.[16]

But even funding NCLB at the levels that Congress originally authorized would leave it light years away from what it would take to realize the promises NCLB makes, even on its own narrow test score terms. William Mathis, a superintendent of schools in Vermont and a professor of education finance at the University of Vermont, has tracked studies of the resources required to reach the NCLB mandates. He examined estimates in nearly twenty states that used a wide variety of methods to calculate such costs. These studies show that it would take about a 30 percent annual increase in current school spending for states to come even close to meeting NCLB's mandates. That's about $130 billion a year, or almost ten times what current funding is for Title I programs.[17]

To date, the much-touted increase in federal spending accompanying NCLB represents about a 1 percent increase in total U.S. school spending. This is one reason that increasing numbers of states have been resisting NCLB as an "unfunded mandate." Some states, like New Hampshire, have done cost-benefit analyses to see if it even makes sense to keep taking federal money. The New Hampshire School Administrators Association estimated that the state will receive about $77 in new federal money for each student, while the obligations imposed by the law will cost at least $575 per student.[18] This in a law that actually includes a provision declaring that states do not have "to spend any funds or incur any costs not paid for under this Act." [19]

By itself, money is necessary, but insufficient for school improvement. But to dramatically raise expectations on schools and students without adequately addressing the costs or fixing the inequalities built into our school funding system is neither fair nor reasonable. Educational excellence in low-performing schools and districts needs to be built on a foundation of educational equity.

There is no denying that NCLB has brought some long overdue attention to the problem of educational inequality. Those of us who wrestle daily with the realities of this inequality in our classrooms and our schools welcome this attention. The problem is that what NCLB proposes to do about this inequality is woefully inadequate to the task, and in some ways, will make things worse. It shines the spotlight on problems it has no strategies for solving and it imposes tests and sanctions that will increase inequality in education rather than reduce it.

The more people see how NCLB actually works, the more it becomes clear that NCLB is not a tool for solving a crisis in public education, but a tool for creating one.[20] Public schools need a very different tool kit for the problems we face.

4: NCLB and Democracy

DEBORAH MEIER

In 1930 there were 200,000 school boards in the United States. Today, with twice as many citizens and three times as many students in our public schools, we have only 15,000. Once one of every 500 citizens sat on a school board; today it's one out of nearly 20,000. Once most of us knew a school board member personally; today it's rare to know one.

During the years I spent on a school board serving a population of more than 100,000 and responsible for twenty different schools, I never expected my fellow citizens to recognize me on the street or to share their concerns with me. I had barely any firsthand knowledge about what went on in most of those schools.

It's no wonder that most citizens aren't concerned about the demise of public education: it's been a long time since education felt like a public enterprise—except for who pays for it.

This shrinkage of public participation in school governance represents an enormous and utterly unnecessary loss—for our kids' learning and their relationship with the adult world, for the status of public education, for the relationship between citizens and their government, and for democracy itself. It's at the heart of what's gone wrong with education and what must be changed.

Yet, oddly enough, the latest cure is to move schools further and further from their publics and put the most important decisions in the hands of a few large test and text publishers acting under the direction of federal mandates—in short, the law known as NCLB.

Suddenly every state in the nation feels obliged to initiate a massive program of standardized tests starting at ever younger grades upon which all critical decisions will hang, as well as comply with particular federally mandated programs for teaching reading, and, over time, math and science and history. A politically selected panel of experts will determine which programs have met the test—immediately ruling out locally designed ones—of "scientific reliability." New York City was thus obliged to change the way 1.2 million children were being taught to read because the federal Department of Education disapproved of its program. Even if it were possible to claim that one pedagogy was superior to another, in the field of education, as in the field of medicine, one solution does not fit all. Depending on other patient characteristics a good doctor would vary the treatment plan; so it is with a good teacher.

The very definition of what constitutes an educated person is now dictated by federal legislation. A well-educated person is one who scores high on standardized math and reading tests. And ergo a good school is one that either has very high test scores or is moving toward them at a prescribed rate of improvement. Period.

All of this has implications for democracy, and not small ones. We worry about "public engagement" and "parent involvement," two new jargony phrases that were invented precisely as we eliminated all the natural ways in which families and citizens were engaged in their schools.

Bigger Is Not Better

The demise of small districts was coincidental with the demise of small schools. The two phenomena together have led to a serious disconnect between young people and adults, between youth culture and adult culture.

There were good reasons to be concerned that small schools might be havens for parochial prejudices, racial bias, and insularity—and that larger consolidated districts would be able to offer greater variety and economies of scale. Both played a role in the demise of small schools and districts, as well as the increasing role of the state and federal government in schools. We were preparing our youngsters for both national and global citizenship; big schools and big districts were often seen as a way of enlarging young people's exposure to a wider range of options and offering them greater expertise and more specialized programs, as well as protecting the rights of minorities.

Furthermore, the increase over the past half-century of state and federal mandates created compliance problems in small and isolated districts. How could a small school offer the kind of library, science labs, sports programs, range of foreign language opportunities, or Advanced Placement options that would be possible in a large school?

But we embarked on that path without considering the costs, either in how adults saw their responsibility for the education of the next generation, or in the growing disconnect between school and community and its impact on children's intellectual, social, and moral development. Citizenship requires a recognition of what it means to be a member of something—and we've forgotten that kids today have precious little experience being members of anything beyond their immediate family and their self-chosen peer group.

Parochialism certainly can stunt kids' growth and impede

their sharing of larger societal norms and concerns. The solution to parochialism, however, isn't to destroy all small communities and institutions in favor of large, anonymous ones. When we look closely, we see that the consolidation and centralization of school districts actually made the problems they were supposed to cure even worse. Rather than expanding young people's sense of membership in the world, consolidation seriously endangered their feeling of community. And it didn't even save money: the evidence suggests that the cost per graduate of small schools is less.

Nor did consolidation lead to other hoped-for outcomes, such as greater ethnic, racial, and social class integration. Our progress on racial separatism has been substantial, if we look back as far as 1930, but in recent years we have been losing ground. As for social class, the big difference is that far more low-income children now attend school for longer periods of time—but rarely together with rich kids. And if they do attend the same schools, they rarely study in the same classes or belong to the same subgroups. For within the new large schools, kids have re-created their own small schools, made up of their like-minded and look-alike peers. You see them in the hallways and lunchrooms and on the playgrounds.

Now, NCLB does not in itself demand the consolidation of districts and the creations of bigger schools. But as I hope to show, it creates an environment in which the purpose and value of small schools is not allowed to flourish. In fact, it undermines small schools' most important educational characteristic: that they are places where citizens and professionals can exercise judgment and build trust.

A World Designed by Strangers

Local communities are in far less danger of narrow parochialism today than in the past. The influence of television, computers and other technology, and the vast youth-savvy world of mass entertainment has altered the landscape of our lives, especially for children.

Few of today's youngsters lack awareness of the larger demands of society, as job requirements and college expectations are largely national in scope. We are inescapably connected by these new technologies, and there are more of them every year. It's not the Big World that kids are cut off from; increasingly, it's the one at their doorsteps—their own communities.

Education has barely acknowledged, much less begun to address, this sea change toward a new world of universalism run amok. We are not much of a match anymore for the educational impact of the national norms established, not by schools, teachers, or churches but by that great equalizer the mass media, with its relentless drive to turn our kids into world-class consumers.

By the time they are adolescents, our children are largely cut off from relationships with adults outside their immediate families—and stuck with one another in a world designed for them by strangers. They all are educated by the music, advertisements, and products designed to sell to an international youth market. They are carefully groomed to recognize ways to enhance their status in the race to look good, get ahead, be the most, have the most. What they do not have are very strong roots in any specific multiage community.

NCLB takes this one giant step forward—pitting every child against every other child to look good and get ahead, and every school against every other school, and it does so with a measurement tool that barely acknowledges anything but test scores as a measure of a sound education.

NCLB is not itself responsible for the divide between adults and children, for the breakdown of multiage communities. It merely locks these into place. Exactly at a time when we need educational policies that will counter these trends, we get NCLB, which instead amplifies their negative effects. It does so in specific ways:

By relying on standardized tests as the only measure of school quality, NCLB usurps the right of local communities to define the attributes of a sound education. Districts are further encouraged to limit any local alternatives by having schools limit their curriculum time to what will prepare children for tests, as is pointed out in the other pieces in this book. This will, again as the other authors have shown, dumb down decades of efforts to provide all children with what was once offered only to the rich—a genuinely challenging and engaging program of study.

By ignoring ample evidence that the psychometric tools of testing provide limited predictions of school success, above all when it comes to children outside the mainstream (children of color, of the poor, those with handicaps or limited English proficiency), NCLB forces local districts to engage in one-size-fits all practices that ignore the needs of these children. Districts will be encouraged to push out these so called non-performers in order to protect their movement toward Adequate Yearly Progress or else risk being labeled a failing school.

By suggesting that public schools can produce equity regardless of social inequity, NCLB sets up local districts for failure. This failure will lead to calls for the ultimate limitation of local, democratic authority, that is, calls for the privatization of our public schools.

Above all, NCLB assumes that neither children, their families, their teachers, nor their communities can be trusted to make important decisions about their schools. It defines such parties as special biased self-interests, whose judgment is inferior to that of the bureaucrats at the Department of Education and the various testing services.

Democracy Is Messy—And That's Good

We need schools where strong cross-generational relationships can be built around matters of importance to the world.
Schools cannot do it alone—kids also need other non-school
communities—but creating such schools is a necessary start.
These schools can exist only in communities that trust them.
There is no shortcut. The authority needed to do the job requires trust. Trusting our schools cannot be a long-term goal
in some utopian vision. If you don't trust the baby-sitter, no
accountability scheme will make it safe to leave your child in
her hands tonight. The only alternative is to stay home.

There is no way around it. We have to work harder at
making our schools and teachers trustworthy. And that, in
turn, means we need schools whose work we can easily see,
whose governors are folks we know well, and whose graduates' lives we can track without complex databases or academic studies.

The business world offers little guidance in this task. The
ways of business hardly work for business, where "buyer be-
ware" is the primary response to demands for accountability.

We need to return schools to our fellow citizens—yes, ordinary citizens, with all their warts. The solution to the messi-
ness of democracy is more of it—and more time set aside to
make it work. If we want to continue our grand experiment
in American democracy, we are stuck depending on the people "to exercise their control with a wholesome discretion,"
in Thomas Jefferson's words. And if they are not enlightened
enough to do so, he said, "the remedy is not to take it from
them, but to inform their discretion by education."

That's what local school boards are intended to be all
about. If we can't trust ordinary citizens with matters of local
K-12 schooling, whatever can we trust them with? And why

would we instead trust presidents and governors or the task forces they select to replace such judgments on matters so close to the raising of our children?

Choice and Voice

How might we go about establishing greater trust? We might start by multiplying, not reducing, the number of local boards, to return to the ratio we once enjoyed. At most no school committee that makes decisions about teaching and learning should have authority over more than perhaps 2,500 students and at most ten small schools. Maybe each school should have its own board.

Trust in schools can't grow unless principals, parents, teachers, and kids know each other well, and their work is accessible to the larger community. Likewise, the board members that oversee them must know the schools intimately —through firsthand engagement, not printouts and manipulatable bureaucratic data.

Like the private and parochial schools that the current federal government seems to favor, Mission Hill School—although part of a larger citywide system in Boston—has its own board, made up of five parent representatives, five staff representatives, five public members chosen jointly, and two students. And while the Boston School Committee has ultimate power, "in-between" (which is most of the time) it's our own board that makes the important decisions on policy, budget, and personnel. That's part of the secret of our success. Maybe each school needs its own form of self-governance.

The state can set broad guidelines, and it can surely demand that schools make their standards explicit and the evidence of performance publicly accessible. It can insist on fairness for all citizens—and set out what such fairness requires. But each local board ought to be responsible for the details, including exactly how schools are held accountable to their constituents and what evidence will count toward the awarding of diplomas. There is precious little likelihood that a board will ignore what colleges and employers say, what the Educational Testing Service and other credentialing bodies lay down as norms, or what the mass media and national politicians and public figures claim needs to be done.

The state might reasonably require that sample populations of students be tested to look at indicators across localities. And it might require schools to submit every few years to a review of their work by a panel of expert and lay outsiders, whose opinions and analysis would be made public. Otherwise, let there be both voice and, where possible, choice—close to where children live. While choice allows folks to vote with their feet, voice allows them to vote in the most democratic sense—by going to the polls.

Both choice and voice strengthen the allegiance of communities to their schools. Not all people will get exactly what they want; but democracy is also all about compromises, building consensus, thinking about the other guy's needs and views, and a commitment to the larger community.

There will be acrimony, and there will be local fights. Hurrah, not alas. It is the habits of mind necessary for practicing and resolving disagreement—the mental toughness that democracy rests on—that kids most need to learn about in school. If we all agreed about everything, we wouldn't need democracy; we wouldn't need to learn how people work out differences.

Local school boards need to look politicians, corporate boards, and foundation leaders square in the eye and remind them: This is what America is all about. And it just so happens it's what a strong and rigorous education requires—even if we don't get it right at first or all the time. That, too, is what America is all about.

Rebuilding Trust

Our school boards need to turn their eyes to their real constituencies—not just to following the dictates of state and federal government bureaucrats.

Good school governance needs to keep its eyes on its real constituents—above all the kids and their families. Disappointing them is what such a board must worry about day and night. What it doesn't need to do is live in fear of state and federal government micromanagers. That's not easy, of course. But it will be the foundation of a powerful coalition of school people and local school boards creating trustworthy schools.

There is no way to give all kids a serious and high-quality education unless and until we make their schools worthy of trust—even as we acknowledge the need for skepticism, openness, review, and feedback. The more these two groups— educators and school boards—act as though they deserve distrust, the less they'll be trusted. The Texas "miracle" has not led to one whit more trust in its schools. No sooner did kids meet the requirements of its tightly controlled state system than new, even tighter controls followed. Teachers in Texas dare not speak out, scripts downloaded daily into their classrooms replace teacher's judgment, and dishonest reporting of results grows amidst secrecy and fear. When all the stakes rest on data that rests in the hands of distant authorities, the data itself becomes less and less reliable. Distrust feeds distrust.

Here's the rub: the same reasons that we need to trust local school boards—for better or worse—apply to how school boards need to relate to the faculties and families in their schools. Micromanaging doesn't work at this level, either. But schools need to accept that asking for explanations and offering tough criticism is not micromanaging. In fact, all professionals need to openly defend their work, even in settings that are essentially supportive. Getting that balance right is difficult, and it won't always work. Some local boards will be too passive and some too active; some will go from one stance to another, depending on the issues.

But it can be done. I've seen it happen, in communities all across this country. There are at least four critical first steps on the road to trust:

1. Build a community-wide consensus about the essential purposes of schools and education—about what comes first. Unlike NCLBs mandate for test scores targeted to full proficiency in 2014, communities should publicly debate, publish, and record their progress toward their own sense of student success. If test scores are a community's answer, then test scores will be its prime object. Even then which test will be a matter of local concern.

2. Agree on what to do about minority viewpoints that can't comfortably fit under the same roof—on how to provide the needed choices. Public bodies can agree to offer choices to its community, as we did in District 4 in Manhattan's East Harlem so many years ago. Opening the door to privatization is not necessary for choice to work. Any accountability plan like NCLB must provide for public choice for schools that will be even more accountable to their self-selected public.

3. Select the key educational leaders to carry out the work in ways that honor the views of both families and professional staff—which in turn means placing such decisions close to the school. (For a bill touted as a comprehensive school reform bill, NCLB itself is—not accidentally—silent on the leadership that good public schools need.) We need to provide these leaders with the kind of respect and freedom they need to do the job. We cannot expect students to respect their elders if we don't. We need political leadership that listens to expertise in the field.

4. Provide equal resources to the rich and poor—in terms of the money we spend on kids as well as the qualifications of their teaching staffs. What we think is required to educate the richest of our citizens' children should be available to the poorest—and then some. Fairness dictates that we spend equal monies on all our children's schooling. Without such equity, No Child Left Behind is just a political slogan.

Of course, even these steps would not in themselves make up for the other gaps in the lives of the most and the least advantaged, nor will they address the impact of the other important educational forces upon the lives of the young. But it's a start.

There are no shortcuts. When we pretend that efficiency means we don't have to get to know each other, when we depend on test scores or other indirect forms of data to avoid having to look closely at what kids are actually doing, we undermine trust. At best, standardized tests measure only a very small portion of what is vital for adult success in contemporary life. They totally ignore vast areas of critical significance (such as oral language, teamwork, reliability, initiative, and judgment). We wouldn't trust a doctor who made life-or-death decisions about our treatment by looking at only one test result or who was not allowed to exercise judgment about what to prescribe for this or that particular situation.

As in medicine, meaningful assessment and diagnosis in education depend on parents and professionals having the time to examine an array of interesting data. School boards need to be engaged in helping the community gather and then understand the data. The data should include that all-too-rare information about what happens to graduates when they become adults. For example, what percentage of young adults vote? Finally, board members and educators should use this information to engage the public in tough and important conversations about our children.

It has never been easy, and it never will be. There are times when expertise overrules popular opinion, and vice versa. But we cannot and will not do a better job of resolving these conflicts by getting rid of the crucial local voice of the people. We cannot hope to raise a generation of thoughtful citizens in schools where adults are not themselves viewed as thoughtful citizens.

Schools need to be governed in ways that honor the same intellectual and social skills we expect our children to master, and—ideally—in ways the young can see, hear, and respect. At every point along the way we must connect the dots between our practice and democracy. It's nice when ends and means can come together in this way, and it's the most powerful form of education when they do. Will it be neat and orderly? Probably not. But democracy is and ever was messy, problematic, and it is always a work in progress.

5: NCLB and the Effort to Privatize Public Education

ALFIE KOHN

If a single, powerful objection is reason enough to oppose a law, then we have multiple justifications for saying no to the legislation that some have rechristened No Child Left Untested:

- *NCLB usurps the power of local communities to choose their own policies and programs. It represents a power grab on the part of the federal government that is unprecedented in the history of U.S. education.*

- *It compromises the quality of teaching by forcing teachers to worry more about raising test scores than about promoting meaningful learning.*

- *It punishes those who most need help and sets back efforts to close the gap between rich and poor, and between black and white.*

These indictments, and others as well, are laid out in the other chapters of this book. But to fully assess the impact of this law, we need to understand it in context. Some of NCLB's most energetic supporters are people and organizations opposed to the whole idea of public schooling—and, indeed, to public institutions in general. Their idea of "reform" turns out to entail some sort of privatization, such that education is gradually transferred to the marketplace. There, the bottom line is not what benefits children but what produces profit.

This shift is portrayed as a bold challenge to the current system, whereas defenders of public education are said to lack the vision or courage to endorse meaningful change—and are accused of being apologists for schooling as it now exists. It's a very clever gambit, you have to admit. Either you're skeptical of public education or you're satisfied with mediocrity.

Let's state what should be obvious, then. First, a defense of public education is wholly consistent with a desire for excellence. Second, by most conventional criteria, public schools have done surprisingly well in managing with limited resources to educate an increasingly diverse student population.[1] Third, notwithstanding that assessment, there's plenty of room for dissatisfaction with the current state of our schools. An awful lot is wrong with them: the way conformity is valued over curiosity and enforced with rewards and punishments, the way children are compelled to compete against one another, the way curriculum so often privileges skills over meaning, the way students are prevented from designing their own learning, the way instruction and assessment are increasingly standardized, the way different avenues of study are rarely integrated, the way educators are systematically de-skilled. . . . And I'm just getting warmed up.

Notice, however, that these criticisms are quite different from—in fact, often the exact opposite of—the particulars cited by most proponents of vouchers and similar "reforms." To that extent, even if privatization worked exactly the way it was supposed to, we shouldn't expect any of the defects I've just listed to be corrected. If anything, such a system-level shift is likely to exacerbate problems at the level of teaching and learning.[2]

"Freedom" from Public Education

I try to imagine myself as a privatizer. How would I proceed? If my objective were to dismantle public schools, I would begin by trying to discredit them. I would probably refer to them as "government" schools, hoping to tap into a vein of libertarian resentment. I would never miss an opportunity to sneer at researchers and teacher educators as out-of-touch "educationists." Recognizing that it's politically unwise to attack teachers, I would do so obliquely, bashing the unions to which most of them belong. Most important, if I had the power, I would ratchet up the number and difficulty of standardized tests that students had to take, in order that I could point to the predictably pitiful results. I would then defy my opponents to defend the schools that had produced students who had done so poorly.

How closely does my thought experiment match reality? One way to ascertain the actual motivation behind the widespread use of testing—which is, of course, the cornerstone of NCLB—is to watch what happens in the real world when a lot of students manage to do well on a given test. Are schools credited and teachers congratulated? Hardly. The response, from New Jersey to New Mexico, is instead to make the test harder, with the result that many more students subsequently fail. Consider this item from the *Boston Globe*:

> As the first senior class required to pass the [state's standardized] MCAS exam prepares for graduation, state education officials are considering raising the passing grade for the exam. State Education Commissioner David Driscoll and Board of Edu-

> cation chairman James Peyser said the passing grade needs to be
> raised to keep the test challenging, given that a high proportion
> of students are passing it on the first try.... Peyser said as stu-
> dents continue to meet the standard, the state is challenged to
> make the exam meaningful.[3]

You have to admire the sheer Orwellian chutzpah represented by that last word. By definition, a test is "meaningful" only if large numbers of students (and, by implication,
schools) fare poorly on it. What at first seems purely perverse—a mindless acceptance of the premise that harder is always better—reveals itself instead as a strategic move in the
service of a very specific objective. Peyser, you see, served for
eight years as executive director of the conservative Pioneer
Institute, a Boston-based think tank devoted to "the applica-
tion of free market principles to state and local policy" (in the
words of the organization's website). The man charged with
overseeing public education in Massachusetts is critical of the
very idea of public education. And how does he choose to pursue his privatizing agenda? By raising the bar until alarming
failure is assured.

(Notice: alarming failure, not universal failure. As education policy makers across the country have learned, there are
political costs to having too many students flunk the tests,
particularly if an unseemly number of them are white and
relatively affluent. At that point, politically potent parents—
and, eventually, even education reporters—may begin to ask
inconvenient questions about the test itself. Fortunately, by
tinkering with the construction of items on the exam and ad-
justing the cut score, it is possible to ensure virtually any out-
come long before the tests are scored, or even administered.
For the officials in charge, the enterprise of standardized testing is reminiscent of shooting an arrow into a wall and then
drawing the target around it.)

Of course, tougher standards are usually justified in the name of excellence—or, even more audaciously given the demographics of most of the victims, in the name of equity. One doesn't expect to hear people like Peyser casually concede that the real point of this whole standards-and-testing business is to make the schools look bad, the better to justify a free-market alternative. Now and then, however, a revealing comment does slip out. For example, in an article that approvingly described Colorado's policy of publishing schools' test scores, the *School Choice Advocate*, the newsletter of the Milton and Rose Friedman Foundation, quoted a senior education advisor to Republican governor Bill Owens as saying that the motive behind reporting these results was to "greatly enhance and build pressure for school choice."[4]

An op-ed by William Bennett and Chester Finn, published in the *Wall Street Journal* at the end of 2003, underscored the integral relationship between the push for high-stakes testing (which they call "standards"), and the effort to undermine public schooling (which they call "freedom"). The latter bit of spin is interesting in its own right: vouchers, having been decisively rejected by voters on several occasions, were promptly reintroduced as "school choice" to make them sound more palatable.[5] But apparently an even more blatant appeal to emotionally charged values is now called for. In any case, the article notes (correctly, I fear) that "our two political parties ... can find common ground on testing and accountability," but then goes on to announce that "what Republicans have going for them in education is freedom." They understand this value "because of their business ties." Unlike Democrats, they are "not afraid of freedom."

Even in an era distinguished by unpleasantly adversarial discourse, Bennett and Finn plumb its lowest depths with the charge that freedom is a "domain that few Democrats dare to visit." (Their evidence for this charge is that most Democrats exclude private schools from choice plans.) But this nasty little essay, headlined "No Standards Without Freedom," serves primarily to remind us that many of the most vocal proponents of accountability—defined, as it usually is these days, in terms of top-down standards and coercive pressure to raise scores on an endless series of standardized tests—have absolutely no interest in improving the schools that struggle to fulfill these requirements. Public education in their view is not something to be made better; it is something from which we need to be freed.

Privatization via NCLB

None of this is exactly new. "Standards" have been used to promote "freedom" for some time. But if that picture has been slowly coming into focus as education policies are enacted at the state level, it now attains digital clarity as a result of federal involvement. Even those observers who missed—or dismissed—the causal relationship up until now are coming to realize that you don't have to be a conspiracy nut to understand the real purpose of NCLB. Indeed, you have to be visually impaired *not* to see it.

Jamie McKenzie, a former superintendent, put it this way on his website, Nochildleft.com: "Misrepresented as a reform effort, NCLB is actually a cynical effort to shift public school funding to a host of private schools, religious schools and free-market diploma mills or corporate experiments in education." The same point has been made by Gerald Bracey, Stan Karp, and a number of others. Lately, even some prominent politicians are catching on. Senator Jim Jeffords, who chaired the Senate committee that oversees education from 1997 to 2001, has described the law as a back-door maneuver "that will let the private sector take over public education, something the Republicans have wanted for years."[6]

So what is it about NCLB in particular that has led a growing number of people to view it as a stalking horse for privatization? While any test can be, and many tests have been, rigged to create the impression of public school failure, nothing has ever come close to NCLB in this regard. Put aside for a moment the rather important point that higher scores on standardized tests do not necessarily reflect meaningful improvement in teaching or learning—and may even indicate the opposite.[7] Let's assume for the sake of the argument that better performance on these tests *was* a good sign. This law's criteria for being judged successful—how fast the scores must rise, and how high, and for how many subgroups of students—are nothing short of ludicrous. NCLB requires every single student to score at or above the proficient level by 2014, something that has never been done before and that few unmedicated observers believe is possible.[8]

As Monty Neill has explained, even the criteria for making "adequate yearly progress" toward that goal are such that "virtually no schools serving large numbers of low-income children will clear these arbitrary hurdles." Consequently, he adds, "many successful schools will be declared "failing" and may be forced to drop practices that work well. Already, highly regarded schools have been put on the "failing" list."[9] Schools that do manage to jump through these hoops, which include a 95 percent participation rate in the testing, must then contend with comparable hurdles involving the qualifications of their teachers.

The party line, of course, is that all these requirements are meant to make public schools improve, and that forcing every state to test every student every year (from third through eighth grades and then again in high school) is intended to identify troubled schools in order to "determine who needs extra help," as President Bush has put it.[10] To anyone who makes this claim with a straight face, we might respond by asking three questions.

1. How many schools will NCLB-required testing reveal to be troubled that were not previously identified as such? For the last year or so, I have challenged defenders of the law to name a single school anywhere in the country whose inadequacy was a secret until yet another wave of standardized test results was released. So far I have had no takers.

2. Of the many schools and districts that are obviously struggling, how many have received the resources they need, at least without a court order? If conservatives are sincere in saying they want more testing in order to determine where help is needed, what has their track record been in providing that help? The answer is painfully obvious, of course: Many of the same people who justify more standardized tests for information-gathering purposes have also claimed that more money doesn't produce improvement. The Bush administration's proposed budgets have fallen far short of what states would need just to implement NCLB itself, and those who point this out are dismissed as malcontents. (Thus Bennett and Finn: "Democrats are now saying that Republicans are not spending enough. But that is what they always say—enough is never sufficient for them when it comes to education spending.")

3. What have the results of high-stakes testing been to this point? To the best of my knowledge, no positive effects have ever been demonstrated, unless you count higher scores on these same tests. More low-income and minority students are dropping out, more teachers (often the best ones) are leaving the profession, and more mind-numbing test preparation is displacing genuine instruction. Why should anyone believe that annual do-or-die testing mandated by the federal government will lead to anything different? Moreover, the engine of this legislation is punishment. NCLB is designed to humiliate and hurt the schools that, according to its own standards, most need help. Families at

those schools are given a green light to abandon them—and, specifically, to transfer to other schools that don't want them and probably can't handle them. This, it quickly becomes clear, is an excellent way to sandbag the "successful" schools, too.

So who will be left undisturbed and sitting pretty? Private schools and companies hoping to take over public schools. In the meantime, various corporations are already benefiting. The day after Bennett and Finn's rousing defense of freedom appeared on its op-ed page, the *Wall Street Journal* published a news story that began as follows: "Teachers, parents, and principals may have their doubts about No Child Left Behind. But business loves it." Apart from the obvious bonanza for the giant companies that design and score standardized tests, "hundreds of 'supplemental service providers' have already lined up to offer tutoring, including Sylvan, Kaplan Inc. and Princeton Review Inc. . . . Kaplan says revenue for its elementary—and secondary—school division has doubled since No Child Left Behind passed."[11]

The Accountability-Privatization Connection

Ultimately, any attempt to demonstrate the commitment to privatization lurking behind NCLB doesn't require judgments about the probability that its requirements can be fulfilled, or speculation about the significance of which companies find it profitable. That commitment is a matter of public record. As originally proposed by the Bush administration, the legislation would have used federal funds to provide private school vouchers to students in Title I schools with lagging test results. This provision was dropped only when it threatened to torpedo the whole bill; instead, the stick used to beat schools into raising their scores was limited to the threat that students could transfer to other public schools.

Since then, Bush's Department of Education has taken other steps to pursue its agenda, such as allocating money hand over fist to private groups that share that agenda. In early 2004, People for the American Way reported that the administration has funneled more than $75 million in taxpayer funds to pro-voucher groups and miscellaneous for-profit entities. Among them is William Bennett's latest gamble, known as K12—a company specializing in on-line education for homeschoolers. (Finn sits on the board of directors.) "Standards" plus "freedom" may eventually add up to considerable revenue, then. Meanwhile, the Department of Education is happy to ease the transition: a school choice pilot program in Arkansas received $11.5 million to buy a curriculum from Bennett's outfit, and a virtual charter school in Pennsylvania affiliated with K12 got $2.5 million.[12]

At the center of the conservative network receiving public funds to pursue an anti-public agenda is the Education Leaders Council (ELC), which was created in 1995 as a more conservative alternative to the Council of Chief State School Officers (which itself is not all that progressive). One of its founders was Eugene W. Hickok, formerly Pennsylvania's Secretary of Education and now the second-ranking official in the U.S. Department of Education. Hickok brushes off the charge that DOE is promoting and funding privatization. If there's any favoritism reflected in these grants, he says, it's only in that "we support those organizations that support No Child Left Behind."[13]

But that's exactly the point. A hefty proportion of those who support vouchers also support NCLB, in large part because the latter is a means to the former. Take Lisa Graham Keegan, who was Arizona's school superintendent and is now ELC's executive director. She was a bit more forthcoming about the grants than Hickok, telling a reporter that it's only natural for the Bush administration to want to correct a "liberal bias" in American education by giving grants to groups that share its philosophy. "It is necessary to be ideological in education these days if you want to promote academic standards, school choice, and new routes to certifying teachers.' "[14] Notice again the juxtaposition of "standards" and "choice," this time joined by another element of the conservatives' agenda: an initiative, undertaken jointly by the ELC and a group set up by Finn's Thomas B. Fordham Foundation—and, again, publicly funded thanks to DOE—to create a new quasi-private route to teacher credentialing.

For that matter, take Education Secretary Rod Paige, who appeared at an ELC conference to assure its members that they were "doing God's work."[15] Earlier, he had spent his years as superintendent in Houston doing anything and everything to raise test scores (or, rather, as another chapter of this book demonstrates, to give the appearance of raising test scores). At the same time, his "tenure as superintendent was marked by efforts to privatize or contract out not only custodial, payroll, and food services, but also educational services like 'alternative schools' for students with 'discipline problems.' "[16]

In January 2004, Paige made his way around the perimeter of the U.S. Capitol to speak at the conservative Heritage Foundation, whose headquarters stand about a dozen blocks from the Department of Education. His purpose was twofold: to laud NCLB for injecting "competition into the public school system" and to point out that vouchers—which he called "opportunity scholarships"—are the next logical step in offering "educational emancipation" from "the chains of bureaucracy."

The arguments and rhetoric his speechwriters employed on that occasion are instructive. For example, he explained that the way we improve education is "one child at a time"— a phrase both more substantive and more dangerous than it may seem at first hearing. And he demanded to know how anyone could oppose vouchers in light of the fact that the GI

Bill was "the greatest voucher program in history." Paige was particularly enthusiastic about the newly passed legislation that earmarks $14 million in public funds—federal funds, for the first time—for religious and private schools in Washington, D.C., which he hoped would turn out to be "a model program for the nation." (However, "this isn't a covert plan to finance private, especially Catholic, schools," he assured his audience. The proof? "Many of the students in Catholic schools are not Catholic.")

Paige couldn't restrain himself from gloating over how the passage of this law represented a triumph over "special interests"—that is, those who just "ask for more money" and want "to keep children in schools in need of improvement." These critics are "the real enemies of public schools." In fact, they put him in mind of France's determined opposition to the Bush administration's efforts to secure UN approval for an invasion of Iraq.[17] (At another gathering, a few weeks later, he compared opponents of the law to terrorists.)[18]

Notice that Paige chose to deliver these remarks at the Heritage Foundation, which publishes "No Excuses" apologias for high-stakes testing while simultaneously pushing vouchers and "a competitive market" for education. (Among its other reports: "Why More Money Will Not Solve America's Education Crisis.") Nina Shokraii Rees, a key education analyst at Heritage who helped draft the blueprint for NCLB and pressed for it to include annual high-stakes testing, is now working for Paige, implementing the plans that she and her group helped to formulate. So it goes for the Hoover Institution in California, the Manhattan Institute in New York, the Center for Education Reform in Washington, and other right-wing think tanks. All of them demand higher standards and more testing, and all of them look for ways to turn education over to the marketplace where it will be beyond the reach of democratic control. Over and over again, accountability and privatization appear as conjoined twins.

To point out this correlation is not to deny that there are exceptions to it. To be sure, some proponents of public schooling have, with varying degrees of enthusiasm, hitched a ride on the Accountability Express. I've even heard one or two people argue that testing requirements in general—and NCLB in particular—represents our last chance to *save* public education, to redeem schools in the public's mind by insisting that they be held to high standards.

But the idea that we should scramble to feed the accountability beast is based on the rather desperate hope that we can satisfy its appetite by providing sufficient evidence of excellence. This is a fool's errand. It overlooks the fact that the whole movement is rooted in a top-down, ideologically driven contempt for public institutions, not in a grassroots loss of faith in neighborhood schools. The demand for accountability didn't start in living rooms; it started in places like the Heritage Foundation. After a time, it's true, even parents who think their own children's school is just fine may swallow the rhetoric they've been fed about the inadequacy of public education in general. But do we really think that the people who have cultivated this distrust, who bellow for more testing, who brush off structural barriers like poverty and racism as mere "excuses" for failure, will be satisfied once we agree to let them turn our schools into test-prep factories?

Collateral Damage

In any event, if we did so we'd be destroying the village in order to save it. No, scratch the conditional tense there: the devastation is already under way. Every few days there is fresh evidence of how teaching is being narrowed and dumbed down, standardized and scripted—with poor and minority students getting the worst of the deal as usual. I have an overstuffed file of evidence detailing what we're sacrificing on the altar of accountability, from developmentally appropriate education for little children to rich, project-based learning for older ones, from music to field trips to class discussions.[19]

Lately, it has become clear that piling NCLB on top of the state testing that was already assuming nightmarish proportions is producing still other sorts of collateral damage. For example, there is now increasing pressure to:

- SEGREGATE SCHOOLS BY ETHNICITY. *A new California study confirms what other scholars had predicted: NCLB contains a "diversity penalty" such that the more subgroups of students that attend a given school, the lower the chance it will be able to satisfy all the federally imposed requirements for adequate progress.*[20]

- SEGREGATE CLASSES BY ABILITY. *While there are no hard data yet, it appears that schools may be doing more grouping and tracking in order to maximize the efficiency of test preparation.*[21] *All children lose out from less heterogeneity, but none more than those at the bottom—yet another example of how vulnerable students suffer the most from the shrill demands for accountability.*

- SEGREGATE CLASSES BY AGE. *Multiage education is reportedly becoming less common now—not because its benefits haven't been supported by research and experience (they have), but because of "grade-by-grade academic standards and the consequences tied to not meeting those targets as measured by state tests."*[22]

- CRIMINALIZE MISBEHAVIOR. *"In cities and suburbs around the country, schools are increasingly sending students into the juve-*

nile justice systems for the sort of adolescent misbehavior that used to be handled by school administrators."[23] There are many explanations for this deeply disturbing trend, including the loss of school-based mental health services as a result of budget cuts. But Augustina Reyes of the University of Houston observes, "If teachers are told, 'Your scores go down, you lose your job,' all of a sudden your values shift very quickly. Teachers think, 'With bad kids in my class, I'll have lower achievement on my tests, so I'll use discretion and remove that kid.' "[24] Moreover, attempts to deal with the kinds of problems for which children are now being hauled off by the police—programs to promote conflict resolution and to address bullying and other sorts of violence—are being eliminated because educators and students are themselves being bullied into focusing on test scores to the exclusion of everything else.[25]

- RETAIN STUDENTS IN GRADE. *The same get-tough sensibility that has loosed an avalanche of testing has led to a self-congratulatory war on "social promotion" that consists of forcing students to repeat a grade. The preponderance of evidence indicates that this is just about the worst course of action to take with struggling children in terms of both its academic and social-psychological effects. And the evidence uniformly demonstrates that retention increases the chance that a student will leave school; in fact, it's an even stronger predictor of dropping out than is socioeconomic status.*[26]

If flunking kids is a terrible idea, flunking them solely on the basis of their standardized test scores is even worse. But that's precisely what Chicago, Baltimore, and now the state of Florida are doing, harming tens of thousands of elementary-school children in each case. And even that isn't the whole story. Some students are being forced to repeat a grade not because this is believed (however inaccurately) to be in their best interest, but because pressure for schools to show improved test results induces administrators to hold back potentially low-scoring children the year before a key exam is administered. That way, students in, say, tenth grade will be a year older, with another year of test prep under their belts, before they sit down to start bubbling in ovals.

Across the United States, according to calculations by Walt Haney and his colleagues at Boston College, there were 13 percent more students in ninth grade in 2000 than there were in eighth grade in 1999.[27] Retention rates are particularly high in states like Texas and North Carolina, which helps to explain their apparently impressive scores on the National Assessment of Educational Progress. The impact on the students involved, most of whom end up dropping out, is incalculable, but it makes schools and states look good in an age when accountability trumps all other considerations. Moreover, Haney predicts, "senseless provisions of NCLB likely will lead to a further increase of 5 percent or more in grade nine retention. And of those who are flunked," he adds, "70 to 75 percent will not persist to high school graduation."[28]

The Dangers of Complying with NCLB

Take a step back and consider these examples of what I'm calling collateral damage from high-stakes testing: a shallower, back-to-basics curriculum; more homogeneity; a retreat from innovations like multiage classrooms; more tracking and retention and harsher discipline. What's striking about these ostensibly accidental by-products of policies designed to ensure accountability is that they themselves are on the wish list of many of the same people who push for more testing—and, often, for vouchers.

In fact, we can add one more gift to the right: by virtue of its definition of a qualified teacher, NCLB helps to cement the idea that education consists of pouring knowledge into empty receptacles. We don't need people who know how to help students become proficient learners (a skill that they might be helped to acquire in a school of education); we just need people who know a lot of stuff (a distinction that might simply be certified by a quasi-private entity—using, naturally, a standardized test). Or, as Bennett and Finn explain things to the readers of the *Wall Street Journal*, "A principal choosing teachers will make better informed decisions if she has access to comparable information about how much history or math or science each candidate knows." This nicely rounds out the "reform" agenda, by locking into place a model that not only deprofessionalizes teachers but confuses teaching with the transmission of facts.

The upshot of all this is that the right has constructed a single puzzle of interlocking parts. They are hoping that some people outside their circle will be persuaded to endorse some of those parts (specific uniform curriculum standards, for example, or annual testing) without understanding how they are integrally connected to the others (for example, the incremental dissolution of public schooling and the diminution of the very idea that education is a public good).

They are succeeding largely because decent educators are playing into their hands. That's why we must quit confining our complaints about NCLB to peripheral problems of implementation or funding. Too many people give the impression that there would be nothing to object to if only their own school had been certified as making adequate progress, or if only Washington were more generous in paying for this assault on local autonomy. We have got to stop prefacing our objections by saying that, while the execution of this legislation is faulty, we agree with its laudable objectives. No. What we agree with is some of the rhetoric used to *sell* it, invocations of ideals like excellence and fairness. NCLB is not a step in the right direction. It is a deeply damaging, mostly ill-intentioned law, and no one genuinely committed to improving public schools (or to advancing the interests of those who have suffered from decades of neglect and oppression) should want to have anything to do with it.

Ultimately, we must decide whether we will obediently play our assigned role in helping to punish children and teachers. Every in-service training session, every article, every memo from the central office that offers what amounts to an instruction manual for capitulation slides us further in the wrong direction, until finally we become a nation at risk of abandoning public education altogether. Instead of scrambling to comply with the provisions of NCLB, our obligation is to figure out how best to resist.

Many parents, according to survey data, haven't been following this policy debate very closely. We need to help them see the reality of NCLB that lies behind the sound bites, how much of a threat it poses to learning, equity, and local control. With educators, meanwhile, who already understand its destructive power, the challenge is to convince them to act on what they know, to take a stand against what hurts kids. Above all, we have to keep in mind that NCLB is not like the weather, a part of life that we have to live with, like it or not. Rather, it is a piece of legislation that can be repealed— and part of a larger political effort that can be exposed and opposed.

To challenge the accountability-and-privatization movement is simultaneously to reaffirm that public schools strengthen a democratic society, in part by benefiting vast numbers of people who didn't fare nearly as well before the great experiment of free public education began. Such schools can enrich lives, nourish curiosity, introduce children to new ways of formulating questions and finding answers. To achieve these goals, and to protect basic rights of the people involved, schools need help from federal, state, and local governments. They need adequate funding and support, and assistance in righting the balance when egregious disparities exist between one place and another. But what our elected officials should *not* be doing is requiring standardized assessments and standardized curricula—for example, dictating how children should be taught to read. The government's role is not to impose crippling mandates and tests, but to work with parents, teachers, and students to help public schools survive and flourish.

PART THREE

Alternatives to NCLB

6: Leaving No Child Behind: Overhauling NCLB

MONTY NEILL

As the impact of the No Child Left Behind legislation continues to unfold across the country, educators and child advocates face the tasks of explaining how NCLB hurts schools instead of helps them and constructing an alternate approach to accountability and improvement. As the preceding chapters of this book show, many education reformers believe that NCLB is a fundamentally punitive law that uses flawed standardized tests to label schools as failures and punish them with counterproductive sanctions. It must be transformed into a supportive law that really promotes school improvement and makes good on the promise to, in the words of the Children's Defense Fund, "leave no child behind." The legislation must be reconsidered and rewritten, particularly in the areas of assessment and accountability. But given the current political climate, this won't be a simple task.

Critics need to present specific, positive alternatives, and the alternatives need to be politically viable options. I hope here to point the way to positive, politically feasible changes in the direction of our national and local policies toward schools.

While opinion polls suggest most people know little about NCLB, key promises within the law have wide support. For example, the law authorizes the federal government to increase funding for the education of low-income students. It mandates that states eliminate the academic "achievement gap" that exists between different groups of students, paying particular attention to the progress of students who historically have not been well served. It requires states, districts, and schools to find ways to educate all students successfully.

Such promises have played a key role in winning support for NCLB from some political and civil rights groups that do not share the Bush administration's agenda of privatization and hostility to public education. Understandably, some child advocates and school reformers, long frustrated with the quality of education for poor students, viewed NCLB as a potential tool to force schools to improve. Being clear about the reasons why NCLB, as currently written, will be unable to fulfill its lofty promises is a key to building a coalition that can force Congress to make changes in the law, and a key to understanding how it should be changed.

Reviewing the Critique

The fundamental promise of NCLB is that it will bring new levels of attention and achievement to students traditionally underserved by schools through a particular system of accountability—a set of evaluations, rewards, and punishments. This book has provided a detailed critique of that system of accountability from a variety of angles. We need remind ourselves of only a few of those critiques to show that NCLB's methods cannot and will not achieve its stated aims.

Underfunding. NCLB's unfunded mandate to eliminate all test-score gaps in twelve years assumes that schools by themselves can overcome the educational consequences of poverty and racism. Not only has the federal government failed to meet the social, economic, and health-related needs of many children, but NCLB itself does not authorize nearly enough funding to meet its new requirements. The Bush administration has sought almost no increase in ESEA expenditures for FY 2005 and the coming year. The funds Congress has appropriated are about $8 billion per year less than Congress authorized. Meanwhile, states are still suffering from their worst budget crises since World War II, cutting education as well as social programs needed by low-income people.

Testing. The one-size-fits-all assessment requirements— annual testing in reading and math and periodic testing in science—and the accountability provisions attached to them are rigid, harmful, and ultimately unworkable. They will promote bad educational practices and deform curricula in significant ways. In the end, they will lower, not raise, standards for most students. For example, the assessment requirements will lead to further devaluing of non-tested subjects like social studies, music, and art. NCLB focuses on large-scale testing, which is a poor tool for diagnosing individual students' needs and for assessing higher-order learning. The provisions of the law are turning large numbers of schools, particularly those serving low-income children, into test-prep programs. The testing regime punishes the teachers who choose to work in the nation's most underresourced schools and fosters the inaccurate view that most of the nation's public schools are failing.

Effects on schools. Estimates by groups such as the National Conference of State Legislators suggest some 70 percent of the nation's schools will be declared "in need of improvement" before the decade is over and thus be subject to escalating sanctions. Florida reported that 87 percent of its schools and all of its districts failed to make "adequate yearly progress" (AYP) in 2002–03. NCLB's test-and-punish approach to accountability is the foundation for an equally ineffective approach to school improvement. The first step toward improving schools, according to NCLB, is to allow parents to transfer their children to a school with higher test scores. But it does not guarantee that classroom seats will be available. In Chicago, 240,000 students are in schools "in need of improvement," but the district says it has only 1,035 spaces. In part, this is because a majority of Chicago schools are not making AYP. New York City transferred many students from failing schools to marginally different schools, drastically increasing class sizes in the receiving schools. The Bush administration has said overcrowding does not matter. In most cities, magnet schools and those with test-score admissions are not available to students who seek to transfer. NCLB does not invest in building new schools in failing districts, nor does it make rich districts open their doors to students from poor districts.

The end stage of "accountability" is to "reconstitute" a school. The law's options include turning it into a charter school, privatizing its management, having the state take it over, or firing the principal and relevant teachers. Not one of the listed options has any meaningful record of success in consistently improving student outcomes. Under NCLB, accountability *mechanisms* reduce education to test preparation, create chaos, and lead toward the destruction of public schooling.

In sum, NCLB's promises are undermined by its realities. The accountability measures institutionalized by the legislation are fundamentally insufficient and counterproductive to the goals of educating all students well and of serving well the underserved.

Principles for Authentic Accountability

Any response to the punitive nature of the NCLB must be balanced by recognition that there is a genuine need for helpful school accountability, particularly for those schools that serve communities of color and economically disenfranchised families. Opposition to NCLB doesn't mean opposing any and all forms of accountability. Rather, the law should be used to advocate for a way to develop genuine accountability that supports improved student learning and schools.

FairTest, a nonprofit organization of which I am director, is collaborating with national and local education, parent, civil rights and community groups, and with researchers to develop new models of accountability that are not based on overreliance on standardized tests. Our first step has been to define basic principles on which accountability should rest. The following ten principles are taken from that conversation, from the work of numerous authors, and from examining states, districts, schools, and projects that are doing a better job.

First, however, we must recognize that any accountability system for schools runs the risk of holding educators and students accountable for factors they cannot control. Schools, most prominently, do not control poverty or the historical consequences of racism. Neither schools nor accountability can solve the accumulated problems of class inequities and racial bias, but school systems can and should be held accountable for doing well what they can control.

1. SHARED VISION AND GOALS. *Accountability must be based on shared vision and goals for education and schools, on agreement about what schools should be and do. Local schools and districts and their communities must be the primary authorities in the accountability process. State government must ensure equity of opportunities and treatment (from teacher quality to health and safety); define, with wide participation, core areas for learning (though specific standards can be left to districts and schools); and intervene when localities are unable to provide a high-quality education even when they have adequate resources. The shared community vision should prioritize what is most im-*

portant in academics and other areas of school life. However, a shared vision often is not present, and schools are often arenas of contesting visions. Thus, processes must be established to enable communities to allow differences or to find a sufficient common ground.

2. ADEQUATE RESOURCES USED WELL. Accountability requires that schools must have adequate resources to do their jobs well. This means the money to hire good teachers and ensure continuing professional development, and to provide books, technology, and supplies, in a comfortable, clean, and hospitable environment, in order to ensure that all children receive an adequate and equitable opportunity to learn. Accountability also requires that schools and districts use their resources fairly and well. Children who need more should be provided with more: equity does not mean the same for all, it means that all children receive what they need to fully develop.

3. PARTICIPATION AND DEMOCRACY. Accountability involves active participation and shared power among key actors—it promotes participatory democracy. Teachers and administrators must be allowed to be professionals, to assume responsibility and thus exercise power to regulate their work as teachers. Parents must be involved in making the key decisions about their children's schooling (and not just choosing the school). Students must be actively engaged in learning to be part of a democratic citizenry and not treated merely as passive recipients of knowledge. The larger community needs to participate in setting the basic goals and purposes of the educational system and evaluating how well they have been met. Because the various actors can have conflicting interests, structures must be created that allow all of them to come to share decision-making power. Participation and democracy also implies respect for the diverse experiences and cultural backgrounds of students and communities.

4. PRIORITIZING GOALS. *Assessment information used in accountability must focus on those areas deemed most important, not those areas that are easiest to measure with inexpensive tools such as standardized tests. The academic assessments used in the accountability process must promote and measure deep, strong learning rather than primarily procedural, factual or surface learning. In academics, they must include all important areas of learning.*

Similarly, holding schools accountable for establishing supportive and caring learning environments for all children must rely on evidence that gets at the most important aspects of such communities of learners. Students are both happier and achieve more in environments that are hospitable and welcoming and where students feel empowered, challenged, motivated, and supported. Unfortunately, too few schools systematically evaluate their climate and culture or attempt to improve by using the results of such information, and NCLB and most state systems are silent on the daily living quality of schools.

5. MULTIPLE FORMS OF EVIDENCE. *Accountability requires the use of multiple forms of qualitative and quantitative evidence from both academic and nonacademic areas to arrive at judgments as to where a student or a school is doing well and where not, and to provide a basis for making improvements. No important academic decision about a student, a teacher, an administrator, a school, or a district should be made solely on one type of evidence, such as standardized test scores. (Several test scores do not constitute multiple forms of evidence.) Standardized test data can help identify some educational problems, but no such exams adequately assess to high-quality standards and provide sufficient information for educators to more effectively teach all their students well. Because teachers must use information to improve instruction, it would be more efficient to ensure high-quality assessment practices by teachers than to focus on*

improving standardized testing to be used by underprepared teachers.

Research, particularly that by Black and Wiliam, has strongly demonstrated that skilled use of feedback to students (formative assessment) may be the single most powerful means of improving learning outcomes available to teachers.[1] For assessment to be most helpful to students, it must be comprehensive and regular enough to provide fine-grained useful information about each student to guide further instruction. Most assessment therefore must be classroom-based and used by well-prepared teachers. Schools and districts must ensure that all teachers are skilled users of formative assessments. Standardized exams should supplement, not supplant or overpower, classroom assessment.

6. INCLUSION. Assessment and accountability must include all students, and all students must be assessed and evaluated with a range of appropriate tools and methods. Inclusion also means that accountability data of all sorts should be broken out by major demographic categories, as NCLB requires for test scores. It may be as important to analyze and report both in-school and out-of-school factors that shape how well students do in school.

7. IMPROVEMENT. The most fundamental characteristic of good schools is good teaching. If accountability is to induce improvement, then professional development—particularly time for teachers to collaborate—must be a regular part of teachers' paid work. Schools and districts must be accountable for implementing procedures for using information to guide decision making by educators, students, parents, and the community to improve the quality of schools and learning.

8. EQUITY. All the principles are designed to foster equity. In particular, improvement includes closing the race and class achieve-

ment gaps and helping to overcome the consequences of poverty and racism. They must be closed not only on standardized tests (which can be taught in ways that boost scores while masking continuing gaps, as was done in Texas) but on the social indicators that prefigure school achievement and on the wider range of academic, personal, and social outcomes that society wants for its children.

9. BALANCE BOTTOM-UP AND TOP-DOWN. *Accountability must be truly bottom-up and top-down, rather than top-down with a pretense of bottom-up, as is usually the case in test-based accountability systems. While it remains unclear how to effectively hold the "top" accountable for providing sufficient resources, we can hold them accountable for conducting business with transparency and substantial educator, parent, and community input. We can expect equitable uses of resources and a sound basis, rooted in educational quality, for policies.*

10. INTERVENTIONS. *Interventions from higher levels of government focus on providing useful assistance and only as a last resort include harsher measures. Even though researchers predict that under NCLB most schools will become subject to sanctions, the law's listed governance changes have no evidence of consistent success. This indicates that firing teachers or changing governance are not paths to meaningful improvement. Intervention should focus on factors that can produce powerful improvement, such as rich professional development, stronger parent involvement, and high-quality classroom assessment.*

If a school has taken steps that plausibly will lead to desired improvement, it must be allowed time for those changes to take effect. (The few years allowed by NCLB will usually be insufficient.) During that time, improvement efforts must be monitored using a range of evidence to determine if implementation is proceeding well and schools are able to use information to effectively adjust their improvement efforts.

An Alternative Model

Practices of some schools, proposals for new systems of assessment and accountability, and policies in a few states that refuse to reduce learning to what can be easily measured with standardized tests all indicate how these principles can be implemented. For example, FairTest collaborated with the Massachusetts Coalition for Authentic Reform in Education (CARE) to develop a model authentic assessment and accountability program based largely on work by Harvard educator Vito Perrone. We then helped a coalition of Chicago organizations develop a similar plan, called the New ERA. The plans rely on three sources of information:

> 1. CLASSROOM-BASED INFORMATION. *Each teacher retains evidence of teaching and learning: assignments, student work, and the teacher's observations of the learning processes, strengths and weaknesses of the students. Teachers use a variety of appropriate assessment methods and tools, including observations, student class and home work, projects, essays, tests, presentations in a variety of formats, and portfolios to summarize and evaluate the evidence of learning. These are the basis for teacher reports, qualitative and numerical, as to each student's progress in meeting state, district or school standards as well as goals the teacher or student may have. Reports about each student would be supported by selected classroom evidence, an approach used, for example, by the Learning Record. This information can be summed up, aggregated across individuals, classrooms, schools, the district and even the state.*
>
> *The states of Maine and Nebraska are currently devising*

state assessment systems that will incorporate local assess-ments and minimize the role of state standardized testing.[2] NCLB does allow such state assessment programs, but is so rigid that Maine decided the local assessments would be greatly damaged if used for NCLB. By including local, particularly classroom-based data, much richer and more useful information can be in-cluded in accountability programs—but even these assessments can be misused in a wrong-headed accountability structure.

2. LIMITED STANDARDIZED TESTING. Testing should be in lit-eracy and numeracy and primarily be used as one means for checking on school level information. Marked discrepancies be-tween test results and schools' classroom-based information would be investigated. No major decisions about students or schools would be based on test scores alone.

3. SCHOOL QUALITY REVIEWS. Independent, well-prepared teams would conduct reviews of every school at about five-year intervals, as is done in England, New Zealand, and the state of Rhode Island. Each school first prepares a self-evaluation. Then the team visits, sitting in on classrooms, shadowing students, in-terviewing students, educators, and parents, reviewing random samples of student work, considering academic, social, and com-munity aspects of school life. The team prepares a report with recommendations, which is given to the school and is available to the public in summary and complete form. Schools respond to the review and use it for planning improvement. Schools having dif-ficulty would be reviewed more frequently, with a focus on im-provement efforts.

Schools set up systems through which teachers look at each other's work and student work in order to improve cur-riculum and teaching. Schools must make time for teachers to do this work, as is done in some other countries.

MONTY NEILL

Each school annually prepares a public report, using quantitative and qualitative evidence, to "paint a picture" of the school. The report summarizes information from the assessments and evaluations and describes how the school uses information to improve, changes it has made, and results over the years. The report describes any particular challenges the school faces and the available opportunities students have for learning, particularly addressing resources needed but unavailable.

Information on learning outcomes are summarized by race, gender, income (poverty), English proficiency, and handicap. The data would be reported when the sample sizes are large enough to be meaningful and individuals are not identifiable. School reports must discuss the progress of the groups for whom data is disaggregated.

School reports also would include data on grade retention, suspensions, graduation rates, and the wide range of internal factors that make a school a hospitable environment or not (e.g., school climate surveys). Preferably, schools would gather information about their graduates, from how well elementary students succeeded in high school, to whether high school graduates attended or graduated from college, to employment, civic participation, or personal satisfaction data. The goal for schools is not only academic success but to enhance the chances of life success.

Democratic participation is essential to these plans. A school's community comes together to evaluate the information and improvement plans. Teachers, administrators, parents, and students can openly discuss the successes and problems and come to agreements on what most needs to improve. In some Chicago schools, the local school councils, which have a parent majority, engage in such discussions.

The CARE and New ERA plans call for intervention in

schools that clearly demonstrate they are not succeeding, according to the multiple measures, for all or for significant portions of their students. The first step is an investigation, particularly through the quality review process. A review must include: relevant factors that may be beyond a school's control (e.g., poverty, mobility), the resources a school has, what it does with its resources, and how it might use resources better.

If needed, the district or state should provide carefully targeted assistance. If a school still does not make progress even with assistance, stronger interventions should take place. However, too little is known about how to make such strong interventions succeed. Therefore, states should develop and implement the stronger actions with caution and keep very close track of what does and does not work so as to learn from them.

Some Questions and Answers About the Plans

Q. *Without firm numerical targets with clear sanctions, won't schools just ignore the process?*
A. This gets to the heart of the improvement issue. First, most educators have substantial knowledge, work hard, and care. They do not always have sufficient knowledge. More important, they often work within systems that are dysfunctional despite strong efforts and motivation. We believe most educators are willing to address problems, but they need support and resources to increase their skills and to reshape dysfunctional systems. They do not need unfair attacks or attempts to de-skill them. Too often, current accountability is, or is perceived by teachers as, a means of attack and blame, while teaching to the test actually lowers teaching skills.

If it is true that teachers are less skilled or motivated than we believe, we are in a quandary that current accountability attempts cannot solve. High-stakes testing does not improve teachers' skills or increase motivation to teach well or to learn more. There is no reason to believe that in a high-stakes testing environment, high-quality applicants will seek to enter the profession, which already faces severe shortages. Teachers are particularly likely to leave schools labeled failing, exacerbating the situation. School improvement needs more than anything else skilled teachers who actively participate in improvement efforts. This state cannot be attained by threats or fear.

Second, we have to ask what our goal is: is it to ensure high-quality educational opportunities for all students, or will low-income and minority-group students be consigned to test preparation for "basic skills" in a process that never gets beyond such basics? The goal of focusing only on tests causes schools to ignore many other academic and nonacademic dimensions, thereby depriving children of the rich range of opportunities and supports they need and deserve. These plans expect states, districts, and schools to engage all students in a wide variety of educational experience and build in means both to obtain evidence showing how well this is being done and to ensure all-around improvement.

Third, the CARE and New ERA plans also provide for transparency: claims of success or progress must be backed up with public, verifiable information. That it will be public will be a spur to taking the process seriously. That it is verifiable is a spur to accuracy, rather than to inflated claims. Evidence based in student work will be far more understandable to the public than are test scores, about which most people understand very little. Samples of high-quality student work can be used to help parents, students, and teachers learn what such work looks like and thus seek to attain similar levels of quality.

All that said, we recognize that for a variety of reasons,

even given adequate resources, some schools may fail to do a good job and will not improve despite publicizing the situation and providing support for improvement. FairTest does not believe such schools should be left to continue to fail their students, and the assessment and accountability plans call for stronger measures if needed. That would occur based on a variety of evidence, not simply test score gains that are of questionable validity and reliability.

Q. *Won't your plan take a long time to implement?*
A: Alternative accountability plans could start truly improving schools more quickly than NCLB, which is having counterproductive effects every day. There also is no evidence for us to believe that NCLB can achieve the goals it sets out to achieve using the tools it uses. In fact, there is no reason to believe that schools serving predominantly low-income children can provide high-quality opportunity for all unless they have a major infusion of resources, and no reason to believe they can succeed unless this country develops as strong a will to solve poverty as it now has to develop tests. Barring such changes, many children will continue to be left behind.

The NCLB goal of all students reaching a level equivalent to "proficient" on the National Assessment of Educational Progress (NAEP) is totally unfeasible in the twelve years allowed by the law. This is indeed unfortunate, but it will not be solved by pretending the impossible can be attained. Researchers such as Robert Linn have pointed out that based on the previous decade of NAEP results, reaching proficiency in reading will take more than a century. Part of the problem is that the NAEP proficiency level is very difficult, and part of the problem is the lack of resources. The NCLB goal will itself "take forever," regardless of rhetoric.

There will be other difficult questions to resolve in practice. How much better can schools do if funding is not adequate and poverty remains extensive? Can accountability procedures avoid blaming schools for things they do not control while holding them responsible for what they can do? At what point and with what evidence should decisions to intervene in a specific school be made? If inflexible numerical triggers lead to "interventions" that undermine real education, will the absence of such triggers allow schools, districts, and states to continue to miseducate some children—or, as we think, will rich sources of information shared publicly both help educators and community improve schools and ensure any necessary interventions? Is there a way to pressure states to foster real equity without scapegoating local schools and districts? What should the role of the federal government be in promoting school improvement, and how much money should the federal government be contributing to education?

Schools and districts taking the approach proposed in this chapter will be more likely to make substantive, real progress on valuable, real-world outcomes than will schools focusing on just boosting test scores. The CARE and New ERA approaches will tap into the energy, talent, and caring of educators and students—the human factor that a test-based approach undermines. That is not to say improvement will happen quickly, but that the results will be superior and reached as quickly as happens with test-based accountability. Real change will happen far faster if the nation decides it really means to leave no children behind and takes appropriate measures, in education and elsewhere.

Building a Reform Campaign

If there is to be any chance of changing this law in the next several years, we will have to build a powerful national alliance among education and civil rights organizations and strengthen our public engagement. Advocates can start by recognizing there is wide public concern around some key components of NCLB:

- *The one-size-fits-all nature of testing.*

- *The unfairness of making decisions about individuals or schools based just on test scores.*

- *The danger of teaching to the test.*

We can demonstrate that the choice between historically inadequate education and test-driven "reform" is a false choice because there are other, better options.

Several national education groups, including the American Association of School Administrators and the National Education Association (NEA) are already focusing on these issues. The NEA's 10,000-member Representative Assembly has overwhelming passed a series of resolutions against high-stakes testing and its misuse in NCLB.

But education organizations cannot do it alone. Individual teachers must take an active and prominent role in educating the public about the law and its negative impact. Public opinion surveys, such as the respected *Phi Delta Kappan* annual poll, conclude that teachers are the most respected voices in education. Teachers can help mobilize the public to support change. Educators especially need to reach out to parents, who are likely to turn to teachers for information.

Parents can speak credibly in public. While educators who oppose flawed accountability programs are termed "anti-accountability," parents are less vulnerable to such labeling. In non-union states, where teachers who speak out can easily be fired, the public role of parents may be more important. Because parents are only occasionally well organized, educator groups may need to provide support to parents, while allowing parents to retain their autonomy.

Civil rights groups also can be a powerful force for changing NCLB. Some spoke out against NCLB when it was in Congress. Few members of the Congressional Black and Hispanic Caucuses voted for the law. Recently, the Children's Defense Fund has raised concerns about the overuse and misuse of tests in NCLB. The educational platforms of the National Conference of Black Legislators and the NAACP both oppose high-stakes testing for individuals and warn against teaching to the test.

To be sure, the civil rights community remains somewhat divided on NCLB. Support from some civil rights activists was important to passage of NCLB. Some view the new federal law as a powerful step toward ensuring that states and districts address long-ignored educational needs that have led to weak education for many students. Sanctions, they say, are necessary to force action. High-stakes tests for schools and districts appear to guarantee some sort of results. Supporters of alternative approaches to accountability will have to demonstrate that our approaches provide genuine accountability and do not have the dangerous pitfalls of test-based accountability.

Over the next few years, an ESEA reform alliance will have to work to resolve these differences. There will need to be intense discussions with not just the national leaders of education and civil rights groups, but with classroom teachers, parents, and community activists. We will have to use principles, examples, research, and reason, backed by political clout, to answer the question, How best can federal government help schools build a *multicultural* democracy of well-educated citizens? We think the principles and models described above provide an excellent starting point—but much more remains to be done. NCLB is a time bomb ticking at the center of the public education system. Unless we want to find ourselves standing amidst the rubble, we need to get to work.

Notes

Preamble: A Reminder for Americans

1. Richard H. Bremner, ed., *Children and Youth in America: A Documentary History* (Cambridge, Mass.: Harvard University Press, 1974), 1806ff.

1. From "Separate but Equal" to "No Child Left Behind"

1. G. Sunderman and J. Kim, *Inspiring Vision, Disappointing Results: Four Studies on Implementing the No Child Left Behind Act* (Cambridge, Mass.: Harvard Civil Rights Project, 2004).

2. J. Novak and B. Fuller, *Penalizing Diverse Schools? Similar Test Scores but Different Students Bring Federal Sanctions* (Berkeley: Policy Analysis for California Education, 2003).

3. L. Darling-Hammond, "What Happens to a Dream Deferred? The Continuing Quest for Equal Educational Opportunity," in *Handbook of Research on Multicultural Education,* 2d ed., ed. James A. Banks (San Francisco: Jossey-Bass, 2004), 607–30.

4. Robert L. Linn, "Accountability: Responsibility and Reasonable Expectations," *Educational Researcher* 32 (2003): 3–13.

5. W. J. Erpenpach, E. Forte-Fast, and A. Potts, *Statewide Educational Accountability Under NCLB* (Washington, D.C.: Council for Chief State School Officers, 2003).

6. Novak and Fuller, *Penalizing Diverse Schools?*; Sunderman and Kim, *Inspiring Vision, Disappointing Results.*

7. C. Clotfelter, H. Ladd, J. Vigdor, and R. Diaz, "Do school accounta-

bility systems make it more difficult for low-performing schools to attract and retain high-quality teachers?" paper presented at the annual meeting of the American Economic Association, Washington, D.C., February 2003.

8. D. DeVise, "A+ Plan Prompts Teacher Exodus in Broward County," *Miami Herald,* 5 November 1999.

9. Darling-Hammond, "What Happens to a Dream Deferred?"

10. Erpenpach et al., *Statewide Educational Accountability Under NCLB.*

11. See Monty Neill's essay in this volume.

12. Richard L. Allington and Anne McGill-Franzen, "Unintended Effects of Educational Reform in New York," *Educational Policy 6* (4) (1992): 397–414; D. N. Figlio and L. S. Getzler, "Accountability, Ability, and Disability: Gaming the System?" National Bureau of Economic Research, April 2002.

13. B. A. Jacob, "The Impact of High-Stakes Testing on Student Achievement: Evidence from Chicago," Working Paper, Harvard University, 2002; W. Haney, "The Myth of the Texas Miracle in Education," *Education Policy Analysis Archives* 8 (41) (2000), http://epaa.asu.edu/epaa/v8n41/.

14. L. Darling-Hammond, "The Implications of Testing Policy for Quality and Equality," *Phi Delta Kappan* (November 1991): 220–25; F. Smith et al., *High School Admission and the Improvement of Schooling* (New York: New York City Board of Education, 1986).

15. Haney, "The Myth of the Texas Miracle in Education"; G. Orfield and C. Ashkinaze, *The Closing Door: Conservative Policy and Black Opportunity* (Chicago: University of Chicago Press, 1991), 139; Smith et al., *High School Admission and the Improvement of Schooling.*

16. Numbers of students enrolled in grade 9 are provided by the Massachusetts Department of Education in their "October 1 reports." Numbers of graduates for classes 1994–2002 were provided by the Massachusetts Department of Education in a table entitled "High School Graduation Rates by Race: 1992–2002." Numbers of graduates for 2003 have not yet been published. Numbers of students in position to graduate are those who passed the MCAS in

both English language arts and math and have thus received "competency determination" (i.e., have received a high school diploma) as reported in the Massachusetts Department of Education's report, "Progress Report on Students Attaining the Competency Determination Statewide and by District," February 2004; as reported at http://www.doe.mass.edu/mcas/2003/results/0204cdprogrpt.pdf.

17. A. Wheelock, School Awards Programs and Accountability in Massachusetts: Misusing MCAS Scores to Assess School Quality, 2003, http://www.fairtest.org/arn/Alert%20June02/Alert%20Full% 20Report.html.

18. M. Dobbs, "Education 'Miracle' Has a Math Problem," *Washington Post,* 9 November 2003.

19. D.J. Schemo, "Questions on Data Cloud Luster of Houston Schools," *New York Times,* 11 July 2003.

20. R. F. Ferguson, "Paying for Public Education: New Evidence on How and Why Money Matters," *Harvard Journal on Legislation* (1991): 465–98; E. Fuller, "Do properly certified teachers matter? A comparison of elementary school performance on the TAAS in 1997 between schools with high and low percentages of properly certified regular education teacher" (Austin: The Charles A. Dana Center, University of Texas at Austin, 1998); E. Fuller, "Do properly certified teachers matter? Properly certified algebra teachers and Algebra I achievement in Texas," paper presented at the annual meeting of the American Educational Research Association, New Orleans, La., 2000.

21. Haney, "The Myth of the Texas Miracle in Education."

22. Darling-Hammond, "What Happens to a Dream Deferred?"

23. Bruce Fuller, "Only the Politicking Gets an 'A,'" *Washington Post,* 1 February 2004.

24. Darling-Hammond, "What Happens to a Dream Deferred?"

25. L. Darling-Hammond and G. Sykes, "Wanted: A National Teacher Supply Policy for Education: The Right Way to Meet the 'Highly Qualified Teacher' Challenge," *Educational Policy Analysis Archives* 11 (33) (September 2003), http://epaa.asu.edu/epaa/v11n33/.

2. A View from the Field

1. A growing body of evidence exists on this topic, the most recent addition to it is M. Gail Jones, Brett D. Jones, and Tracy Y. Hargrove, *The Unintended Consequences of High Stakes Testing* (Lanham, Md.: Rowman and Littlefield Publishers, 2003).

2. National Board on Education, Testing, and Public Policy, *High-Stakes Testing and High School Completion,* Boston, January 2004.

3. National Board on Education, Testing, and Public Policy, *The Educational Pipeline,* Boston, January 2004.

4. CBS News, *60 Minutes,* 7 January 2004.

5. "Schools Pressured to Dump Bad Students," *Chicago Sun Times,* 9 January 2004.

6. Siegfried Engelmann and Elaine C. Bruner, *Storybook* 1 (Columbus, Ohio: SRA/McGraw Hill, 1995), 62–63.

7. Jon Vuocolo, "Science Expert Critical of Tests," *Trenton Times,* 27 July 2003.

8. Michael Winerip, "Moving Quickly through History, *New York Times,* 18 June 2003.

9. Associated Press, "Schools Drop Naptime for Testing Preparation," 3 October 2003.

10. Kevin Moran, "Pushing for Play at Galveston ISD," *Houston Chronicle,* 20 November 2003.

11. Erika Chaves, "Field Trips Find Wings Clipped," *Sacramento Bee,* 2 January 2004.

12. Barbara Behrendt, "FCAT goals choke out farming classes," *St. Petersburg Times,* 5 October 2003.

13. "Beating the Bubble Test," *Time,* 1 March 2004.

14. Amy Hetzner, "Take a Test, Get a Prize," *Milwaukee Journal Sentinel,* 8 November 2003.

15. Carolyn Moreau, "Principal Calls Rating 'Grossly Unfair,'" *Hartford Courant,* 22 August 2003.

16. L. McNeil and A. Valenzuela, "The Harmful Impact of the TAAS System of Testing in Texas: Beneath the Accountability Rhetoric," in *Raising Standards or Raising Barriers? Inequality and High Stakes Testing in Public Education*, ed. M. Kornhaber and G. Orfield (New York: Century Foundation, 2001), 127–50.

3. NCLB's Selective Vision of Equality

1. John Novak and Bruce Fuller, "Penalizing Diverse Schools?' PACE Policy Brief, December 2003.

2. Erik W. Robelen, "State Reports on Progress Vary Widely," *Education Week,* 3 September 2003.

3. Monty Neill, "Leaving Children Behind," *Phi Delta Kappan,* November 2003.

4. William Mathis, "No Child Left Behind: Costs and Benefits," *Phi Delta Kappan,* May 2003.

5. Joetta L. Sack, "The Funding Fix: Special Education in an Era of Standards," *Education Week*, 8 January 2004.

6. See U.S. Department of Education press releases for 9 December 2003 and 19 February 2004.

7. See "Battles Ahead Over NCLB," *Philadelphia Inquirer,* 18 November 2003; Maryland Humanities Council, "A Cause for Concern—History Education in Maryland," April 2003; and National Arts Education Association, "Tips for Parent Advocacy," October 2003.

8. Lynn Olson, "In Wake of ESEA, School Data Flowing Forth," *Education Week,* 10 December 2003; "Inadequate Yearly Gains Predicted," *Education Week,* 3 April 2002.

9. All figures from U.S. Census Bureau, adjusted for 2002 dollars.

10. See U.S. Census Bureau, *Health Insurance Coverage in the United States,* 2002; Children's Defense Fund, "Facts on Child Poverty in America," 2002.

11. Educational Testing Service, "Parsing the Achievement Gap," October 2003.

12. Valerie E. Lee and David T. Burkam, "Inequality at the Starting

Gate: Social Background Differences in Achievement as Children Begin School," Economic Policy Institute, 2002.

13. Erik Ness, "Getting the Lead Out," *Rethinking Schools,* Winter 2003.

14. Economic Policy Institute, 2002.15. "The Other Gap, Poor Students Receive Fewer Dollars," Education Trust Data Bulletin, 6 March 2001. The dollar figures refer to gaps in spending between districts that serve the highest percentage of poor students and those that serve the smallest percentage of poor students.

16. Mathis, "No Child Left Behind: Costs and Benefits." 17. *The Federal No Child Left Behind Act: What Will It Cost States* by William Mathis, *Spectrum: The Journal of State Government,* Spring, 2004

18. Mathis, "No Child Left Behind: Costs and Benefits."

19. No Child Left Behind Act, Title IX, Part E, Subpart 2, Sec. 9527; See also Associated Press, "New Federal Education Law Strains State Coffers," 18 April 2003.

20. See Danny Rose, "The Accountability Trap: How 'No Child Left Behind' Creates Crises in Public Schools," *Online Journal,* August 2003.

5. NCLB and the Effort to Privatize Public Education

1. See David C. Berliner and Bruce J. Biddle, *The Manufactured Crisis: Myths, Fraud, and the Attack on America's Public Schools* (Reading, Mass.: Addison-Wesley, 1995); Richard Rothstein, *The Way We Were?: The Myths and Realities of America's Student Achievement* (New York: Century Foundation Press, 1998); and various writings by Gerald Bracey.

2. Making schools resemble businesses often results in a kind of pedagogy that's not merely conservative but reactionary, turning back the clock on the few changes that have managed to infiltrate and improve classrooms. Consider the stultifyingly scripted lessons and dictatorial discipline that pervade for-profit charter schools. Or have a look at some research from England showing that "when schools have to compete for students, they tend to adopt 'safe,' conventional and teacher-centered methods, to stay close to the prescribed curriculum, and to tailor teaching closely to test-taking." (Kari Delhi, "Shopping for Schools," *Orbit* 25, no. 1 [1998]: 32, pub-

lished by the Ontario Institute for Studies in Education at the University of Toronto. The author cites three studies from the UK in support of this conclusion.)

3. C. Kalimah Redd, "Raising of MCAS Bar Is Weighed," *Boston Globe,* 30 April 2003.

4. "In the Spotlight: Colorado," *The School Choice Advocate,* December 2001, 7. Available at www.friedmanfoundation.org/resources/publications/advocate/dec2001_1.pdf.

5. For an account of the carefully coordinated decision to stop using the V-word, see Darcia Harris Bowman, "Republicans Prefer to Back Vouchers by Any Other Name," *Education Week,* 31 January 2001.

6. The McKenzie quotation is from "The NCLB Wrecking Ball," an essay first posted on www.nochildleft.com in November 2003. The Jeffords quotation is from Sally West Johnson, "Mathis Rips Feds Over School Act," *Rutland* (Vermont) *Herald,* 5 February 2003.

7. See, for example, my book *The Case Against Standardized Testing: Raising the Scores, Ruining the Schools* (Portsmouth, N.H.: Heinemann, 2000).

8. See Robert L. Linn, 2003 presidential address to the American Educational Research Association, "Accountability: Responsibility and Reasonable Expectations," available at www.aera.net/pubs/er/pdf/vol32_07/AERA320701.pdf.

9. Monty Neill, "Leaving Children Behind," *Phi Delta Kappan,* November 2003, 225–26.

10. Bush is quoted in Eric W. Robelen, "Bush Marks School Law's 2nd Anniversary," *Education Week,* 14 January 2004, 20.

11. June Kronholz, "Education Companies See Dollars in Bush School-Boost Law," *Wall Street Journal,* 24 December 2003.

12. The report by People for the American Way, "Funding a Movement," is available at www.pfaw.org/pfaw/dfiles/file_259.pdf.

13. Michael Dobbs, "Critics Say Education Dept. Is Favoring Political Right," *Washington Post,* 2 January 2004.

14. Ibid.

15. Quoted in Joetta L. Sack, "ELC Receives Grant to Craft Tests to Evaluate Teachers," *Education Week*, 10 October 2001. On another occasion, Paige commented that "the worst thing that can happen to urban and minority kids is that they are not tested" (quoted in Robert C. Johnston, "Urban Leaders See Paige as 'Our Own,'" *Education Week*, 7 February 2001).

16. Stan Karp, "Paige Leads Dubious Cast of Education Advisors," *Rethinking Schools*, Spring 2001, 4.

17. Paige's January 28, 2004, speech, "A Time for Choice," is available at www.ed.gov/news/speeches/2004/01/01282004.html.

18. Here Paige was referring to the National Educational Association, which he likened to "a terrorist organization" because it opposes some provisions of NCLB. He apologized, under pressure, for a poor choice of words but then immediately resumed his virulent criticisms of the union. See Robert Pear, "Education Chief Calls Union 'Terrorist,' Then Recants," *New York Times*, 24 February 2004.

19. Among many other sources, see M. Gail Jones, Brett D. Jones, and Tracy Hargrove, *The Unintended Consequences of High-Stakes Testing* (Lanham, Md.: Rowman & Littlefield, 2003); and the examples cited at www.susanohanian.org.

20. See John R. Novak and Bruce Fuller, *Penalizing Diverse Schools* (University of California at Berkeley and Stanford University, Policy Analysis for California Education, December 2003). Available at http://pace.berkeley.edu/policy_brief_03-4_Pen.Div.pdf.

21. "The federal No Child Left Behind Act demands that schools show proficient test scores for every student. One approach to achieve that, some argue, is to tailor instruction in groups of similarly skilled students." Laura Pappano, "Grouping Students Undergoes Revival," *Boston Globe*, 14 December 2003.

22. Linda Jacobson, "Once-Popular 'Multiage Grouping' Loses Steam," *Education Week*, 10 September 2003, 1, 15.

23. Sara Rimer, "Unruly Students Facing Arrest, Not Detention," *New York Times*, 4 January 2004.

24. That explanation also makes sense to Mark Soler of the Youth Law Center, a public interest group that protects at-risk children:

"Now zero tolerance is fed less by fear of crime and more by high-stakes testing. Principals want to get rid of kids they perceive as trouble." Both Reyes and Soler are quoted in Annette Fuentes, "Discipline and Punish," *The Nation,* 15 December 2003, 17–20.

25. Scott Poland, a school psychologist and expert in crisis intervention, writes: "School principals have told me that they would like to devote curriculum time to topics such as managing anger, violence prevention and learning to get along with others regardless of race and ethnicity, but . . . [they are] under tremendous pressure to raise academic scores on the state accountability test." Poland, "The Non-Hardware Side of School Safety," NASP (National Association of School Psychologists) *Communique* 28, no. 6 (March 2000). Poland made the same point while testifying at a congressional hearing on school violence in March 1999—a month before the shootings at Columbine.

26. See, for example, the studies cited in Jay P. Heubert, "First, Do No Harm," *Educational Leadership*, December 2002–January 2003, 27.

27. That's triple the rate for the disparity between ninth and eighth grade during the 1970s. See Walt Haney et al., *The Education Pipeline in the United States, 1970–2000* (Boston: National Board on Educational Testing and Public Policy, January 2004). Available at www .bc.edu/research/nbetpp/statements/nbr3.pdf.

28. Walt Haney, personal communication, 15 January 2004. Haney's study also found that there was a substantial drop in high school graduation rates, beginning, as a reporter noticed, "just as President Bill Clinton and Congress ushered in the school accountability measures [that were later] strengthened in the No Child Left Behind Act." Haney is quoted in that same article as saying, "The benign explanation is that this whole standards and reform movement was implemented in an ill-conceived manner." Diana Jean Schemo, "As Testing Rises, 9th Grade Becomes Pivotal," *New York Times*, 18 January 2004. This, of course, invites us to consider explanations that are less benign.

6. Leaving No Child Behind

Portions of this chapter first appeared in Monty Neill, "Making Lemons from Lemonade," *Rethinking Schools*, Fall 2003 (www.rethink ingschools.org) and in a FairTest report on the first two years of NCLB implementation, available on the Web at www.fairtest.org. FairTest led the National Forum on Assessment in producing *Principles and Indicators for Student Assessment Systems*, on which I also relied for this chapter. It is available from FairTest in print for $10 and on the Web at www.fairtest.org/princind.htm.

For more on NCLB, see the FairTest website's National Testing section and back issues of the *Examiner* newsletter. On our Assessment Reform Network page, find state contacts, and three relevant sections: "The Case Against High-Stakes Testing," "The Case for Authentic Assessment," and "Accountability" (look in particular for the articles by Ken Jones and Terry Crooks).

1. Paul Black, and Dylan Wiliam, "Inside the Black Box: Raising Standards Through Classroom Assessment," *Phi Delta Kappan* 80, no. 2 (October 1998): 139–44, 146–48; www.pdkintl.org/kappan/karticle .htm.

The CARE plan: www.fairtest.org/arn/masspage.html

The New Era plan: www.pureparents.org./ ERAplanAug00email.htm

The Learning Record: www.learningrecord.org.

2. Information on Nebraska STARS program can be found in Chris W. Gallagher, "Turning the Accountability Tables: Ten Progressive Lessons from One 'Backward' State," *Phi Delta Kappan* 85, no. 5 (January 2004), www.pdkintl.org/kappan/k0401gal.htm. The state's assessment website is www.nde.state.ne.us. Maine's website: www .state.me.us/education/homepage.htm; see Standards and Assessment. See also the Class Primer at www.elm.maine.edu/assess ments/class/primer/.

Contributors

Linda Darling-Hammond is Charles E. Ducommun Professor of Education at Stanford University School of Education, where she serves as principal investigator for the School Redesign Network and the Stanford Educational Leadership Institute as well as faculty sponsor for the Stanford Teacher Education Program. She was the founding executive director of the National Commission on Teaching and America's Future, which produced in 1996 the widely cited blueprint for education reform, *What Matters Most: Teaching for America's Future*. Darling-Hammond's research, teaching, and policy work focus on educational policy, teaching and teacher education, school restructuring, and educational equity. Among her more than two hundred publications is *The Right to Learn*, recipient of the 1998 Outstanding Book Award from the American Educational Research Association, and *Teaching as the Learning Profession*, awarded the National Staff Development Council's Outstanding Book Award in 2000.

Stan Karp has been a public school teacher in Paterson, New Jersey, for over twenty-five years. He has taught English and journalism to high school students and is currently the lead teacher of the Communications Academy, a small school restructuring project, and a facilitator for his school's "whole school reform" efforts. Karp is also an editor of the journal *Rethinking Schools* and has written widely on issues of school reform and education policy. His articles have appeared in *Education Week*, *Educational Leadership*, and *The National Catholic Reporter*. He is a coeditor of *Funding for Justice: Money, Equity and the Future of Public Education*; *Rethinking Our Classrooms: Teaching for Equity and Justice*; and the recently published *Rethinking School Reform: Views from the Classroom*. He is also a founding member and past co-chair of the National Coalition of Education Activists, a multiracial network of parents, teachers, and education advocates working for reform and equity in public education.

Alfie Kohn is the author of nine books on education and human behavior, including *Punished by Rewards; The Schools Our Children Deserve*; and, most recently, *What Does It Mean to Be Well Educated? And More Essays on Standards, Grading, and Other Follies*. He has been described by *Time* magazine as "perhaps the country's most outspoken critic of education's fixation on grades [and] test scores." A former teacher, he now works with educators across North America and speaks regularly at national conferences.

Deborah Meier, forty years in public education, is currently co-principal of Mission Hill, a public school in Boston; she is the founder of several New York City public schools. Meier is the author of *In Schools We Trust: Creating Communities of Learning in an Era of Testing and Standardization* and *The Power of Their Ideas: Lessons for America from a Small School in Harlem*.

Monty Neill, Ed.D., is the executive director of the National Center for Fair & Open Testing (FairTest), the nation's only organization focused exclusively on assessment reform. He has directed FairTest's work on testing in public schools since 1987 and has taught and administered in preschool, high school, and college. The grandfather of three, Neill has published and spoken widely on assessment issues. His many publications include "Leaving Children Behind: How No Child Left Behind Will Fail Our Children" (*Phi Delta Kappan*, Nov. 2003), *Implementing Performance Assessments: A Guide to Classroom, School, and System Reform*, and *Testing Our Children: A Report Card on State Assessment Systems*, the first comprehensive evaluation of all the state testing programs. He also led the National Forum on Assessment in producing *Principles and Indicators for Student Assessment Systems*, which has been signed by more than eighty national and local education and civil rights organizations. He earned his doctorate from Harvard University with the dissertation, *The Struggle of Boston's Black Community for Quality and Equality in Education: 1960–1985*.

Theodore R. Sizer is University Professor emeritus at Brown University and is currently visiting professor of education at Harvard and Brandeis Universities. He has taught in secondary schools in the U.S. and Australia; was the headmaster of Phillips Academy, Andover, during the 1970s; and was a founder and acting co-principal of the Francis W. Parker Charter Essential School in Devens, Massachusetts, in the 1990s. He served as dean of the Harvard Graduate School of Education from 1964 to 1972 and is the founder of the Coalition of Essential Schools. Sizer is also the author of several books about secondary education, including *Horace's Compromise: The Dilemma of the American High School*.

George H. Wood is the principal of Federal Hocking High School in Stewart, Ohio, and director of The Forum for Education and Democracy. Among his other books are *Schools That Work* (Dutton, 1992) and *A Time to Learn* (Dutton, 1998).

This volume is a project of the Forum for Education and Democracy in collaboration with Beacon Press. The authors have donated all royalties from the work to The Forum.

The Forum is devoted to strong public schools for a strong democracy. We work to promote a wise and engaged democratic citizenry based on the following principles:

- *Responsive public schools with high-quality educators*

- *Equitable and adequate school resources for all children*

- *Appropriate and responsible democratic control of local schools and districts*

- *An education for all students essential to working, living, and contributing to a self-renewing and participatory democracy*

To these ends The Forum commissions papers, provides information on promising practices, comments on educational policy, and works in collaboration with individuals and organizations committed to aims similar to its own. The pieces in this volume represent the views of the authors as individuals and The Forum is pleased to provide this opportunity for them to speak out on these issues that affect our capacity to educate for democratic life.